D1367967

MICHELIN
GUIDE

WASHINGTON DC

DEAR READER,

We are thrilled to launch our very first MICHELIN guide to Washington DC! As part of our meticulous and highly confidential evaluation process, our inspectors have anonymously eaten through the District to compile the finest in each category. As expertly trained food industry professionals, we remain consumer-driven and provide extensive choices to accommodate your comfort, tastes, and budget. The inspectors dine as "regular" customers to experience the same level of service and cuisine as every guest. For this debut edition, we have applied our criteria to reflect some of the more current and diverse elements of DC's dining scene. Besides our famous Stars and Bib Gourmands, don't miss the "Small Plates," highlighting places with distinct service, setting and menu, as well as the impressive choices at great value for "Under $25."

As we take consumer feedback seriously, please contact us at: michelin.guides@michelin.com. You may also follow our Inspectors on Instagram @michelininspectors as they chow their way around the District and other cities.

Our company's founders, Édouard and André Michelin, published the first MICHELIN guide to France in 1900, to provide motorists with practical information about where they could service their cars, find quality lodging, and a good meal. In 1926, the star-rating system was introduced, and over the decades we have developed many new improvements. The team here eagerly carries on these traditions. We truly hope that the MICHELIN guide will remain your preferred reference to Washington DC's restaurants.

→

TABLE OF CONTENTS

THE MICHELIN GUIDE'S COMMITMENTS

EXPERIENCED IN QUALITY!

Whether they are in Japan, the USA, China or Europe, our inspectors apply the same criteria to judge the quality of each and every hotel and restaurant that they visit. The Michelin guide commands a worldwide reputation thanks to the commitments we make to our readers – and we reiterate these below:

→ ANONYMOUS INSPECTIONS

Our inspectors make anonymous visits to restaurants to gauge the quality of cuisine offered to the everyday customer. They pay their own bill and make no indication of their presence. These visits are supplemented by comprehensive monitoring of information—our readers' comments are one valuable source, and are always taken into consideration.

→ INDEPENDENCE

To remain totally objective for our readers, the selection is made with complete independence. Entry into the guide is free. All decisions are discussed with the Editor and our highest awards are considered at a European level.

→ SELECTION & CHOICE

The Guide offers a selection of the best restaurants in each category of comfort and price. A recommendation in the Guides is an honor in itself, and defines the establishment among the "best of the best."

Our famous one ❀, two ❀❀ and three ❀❀❀ Stars identify establishments serving the highest quality cuisine--taking into account the quality of ingredients, the mastery of techniques and flavours, the levels of creativity and, of course, consistency.

→ ANNUAL UPDATES

All practical information, the classifications, and awards, are revised and updated every year to ensure the most reliable information possible.

→ CONSISTENCY & CLASSIFICATIONS

The standards and criteria for the classifications are the same in all countries covered by the Michelin Guides. Our system is used worldwide and easy to apply when selecting a restaurant.

→ OUR AIM

As part of Michelin's ongoing commitment to improving travel and mobility, we do everything possible to make vacations and eating out a pleasure.

HOW TO USE THIS GUIDE

STARS

☆ One Star • High quality cooking, worth a stop

☆☆ Two Stars • Excellent cooking, worth a detour

☆☆☆ Three stars • Exceptional cuisine, worth a special journey

BIB GOURMAND

☺ Inspectors' favorites for good value

CUISINE TYPE

Each entry now comes with a cuisine type, making it quick and easy to identify the food that it serves.

CLASSIFICATION

Restaurant Classifications by Comfort.
More pleasant if in red.

🍽	Small plates
X	Comfortable
XX	Quite comfortable
XxX	Very comfortable
XxxX	Top class comfortable
XxXxX	Luxury in the traditional style

JALEO ☺

SPANISH

XX �&. 🍴

José Andrés's whimsical tapas take center stag
one of three in the metro area. Sure, it has been o
but there are no cobwebs in need of a dusting
irreverent, these are not your papa's tapas. Croq
to a golden-brown and stuffed with ground chi
served in a resin reproduction of a Converse CI
unique and amusing presentation.

DC denizens can even get a taste of El Bulli's trade
style of cooking since Andrés and Ferran Adrià w
Andrés spent time at El Bulli. To that end, be su
olives, which make for a delicious conversation s

■ 480 7th St. NW (at E St.)
METRO: Gallery Pl-Chinatown
PHONE: 202-628-7949 — WEB: www.jale
■ Lunch & dinner daily

FACILITIES & SERVICES

🍷	Notable wine list	🥢	Dim sum
🍶	Notable sake list	ᕒ	Wheelchair accessible
🍸	Notable cocktail list	🍴	Outdoor dining
🍺	Notable beer list	⇆	Private dining room
🍳	Breakfast	🚗	Valet parking
☕	Brunch	💵	Cash only

LOCATING THE ESTABLISHMENT

Location and coordinates on the maps (at the end of the guide), with main sights.

MAP: 3-B4

tpost of Jaleo,
r two decades,
tive, edgy, and
ollo are crisped
échamel, then
sneaker for a

ce experiment-
od chums and
e Adrià's liquid

PRICE: $$

35

MASSERIA ✿

ITALIAN

XX & 🛋 🥂 🍷

MAP: 8-A1

its chic and seamless blend of indoor and outdoor space, Masseria
clear departure from its rough-and-tumble neighborhood. The
ic former warehouse—complete with the requisite exposed ducts,
rete floors, and brick walls—has been glammed up with a stainless
exhibition kitchen, chrome and leather furnishings, pendant lights
ended from nautical rope, and an impressive glass-encased wine cellar.

ll very relaxed, albeit in a well-dressed way, and the feel-good vibe
nds to the staff, who clearly like working here as much as diners enjoy
ring over the multi-course meals.

chef's Puglian heritage comes through in the menu, which features
e to five courses, along with a nightly tasting menu. The kitchen hits all
ight notes balancing trendy and serious. Begin with a cigar box filled
focaccia so sinfully delicious, you'll be tempted to scarf it all down—but
t. You'll want to save room for the spicy fish stew, a thing of beauty
tically brimming with tripe and lobster, or house-made *maccheroni*
thick and gamey goat ragú. Even dessert strays far from the pack,
casing beet ice cream instead of the classic tiramisu.

■ 1340 4th St. NE. (bet. Neal Pl. & Penn St.)
METRO: NoMa-Gallaudet U
PHONE: 202-608-1330 — **WEB:** www.masseria-dc.com
■ Dinner Tue – Sat

PRICE: $$$

45

AVERAGE PRICES

⌘	Under $25
$$	$25 to $50
$$$	$50 to $75
$$$$	Over $75

9

RESTAURANTS

ACADIANA

SOUTHERN

XX 🛖 🛋 🎨 🍽

MAP: 3-A2

With its classic take on N'Awlins fare (think fried green tomatoes, turtle soup, and charbroiled oysters) Acadiana spices things up—way up—in a neighborhood best known for its convention center and business-minded clientele. Begin with a fluffy biscuit topped with sweet-hot red pepper jelly before tucking into one of the Creole or Cajun classics like jambalaya or smoked chicken and andouille sausage gumbo. The kitchen's take on shrimp and grits, dolled up with strips of tender Tasso ham and a crispy-gooey cheddar cheese-grit cake, takes the Southern staple to bold new levels.

And though we wouldn't dare tell mama, the buttery pecan pie, topped with vanilla ice cream and layered with roasted pecans and caramel, is every bit as good as hers.

■ 901 New York Ave. NW (at 9th St.)
METRO: Mt Vernon Sq
PHONE: 202-408-8848 — **WEB:** www.acadianarestaurant.com
■ Lunch Sun – Fri   Dinner nightly
                                                                PRICE: $$

AL TIRAMISU

ITALIAN

X

MAP: 1-B2

With two decades under its belt, it's clear that Al Tiramisu is no flash in the pan. The unassuming restaurant is classic Italian down to the paintings of the Old Country and shelves lined with homemade limoncello. And, for the crowd of diplomats and intellectuals who flock here, these anything-but-trendy environs are precisely the draw.

Though the food is rustic at its core, presentation is nothing if not elegant; and Chef Luigi Diotaiuti's dedication to ingredients has been recognized by DC Slow Food. Menu highlights include toothsome pappardelle tossed with sliced portobello mushrooms in a deliciously savory sauce, as well as grilled fish, lamb chops, and roast chicken. Whatever you choose, be sure to save room for the namesake—and just right—tiramisu.

■ 2014 P St. NW (bet. Hopkins & 20th Sts.)
METRO: Dupont Circle
PHONE: 202-467-4466 — **WEB:** www.altiramisu.com
■ Lunch Mon – Fri   Dinner nightly
                                                                PRICE: $$

AMBAR

BALKAN

MAP: 4-C2

Come armed with an appetite, as there are over 40 small plates and the reasonably priced "Balkan Experience" offers unlimited servings. Though this cuisine is known to be hearty, the kitchen isn't heavy-handed and presents an enticing lineup.

The *ćevapi* piles smoky, succulent minced beef and pork kebabs onto a thin slice of charred flatbread and christens it with a swipe of *kajmak*, a funky sour Balkan cheese. *Pita sa sirom* takes impossibly paper-thin phyllo and layers it with a crumbly, salty cheese and egg filling. The parade of cured meats, flatbreads, salads, and sausages should all be washed down with *rakia*, a classic spirit made from quince or plum. Just in case you thought it would be easy to pick, there are more than 30 varieties on the menu.

■ 523 8th St. SE (bet. E & G Sts.)
METRO: Eastern Market
PHONE: 202-813-3039 — **WEB:** www.ambarrestaurant.com
■ Lunch & dinner daily

PRICE: $$

ANXO

BASQUE

MAP: 2-D4

This Cider House rules. Anxo focuses on cider and small plates hailing from Spain's Basque region. Downstairs, the *pinxtos* bar and wood cask lend a fun, traditional flair, while upstairs has a raw, industrial-meets-rustic appearance. And speaking of which, *pinxtos* (an offering of bite-sized tapas) may include marinated mussels, *bacalao* fritters, oyster mushroom-stuffed piquillos, *chistorra* sausage and aged Manchego among others. The local heirloom red and yellow tomato salad with shaved onion and balsamic vinegar is simply delicious. Stuffed *txipiron* (squid) is set over caramelized onions, while the Onaga red snapper *escabeche,* grilled *à la plancha*, rests in a deliciously tart marinade.

Not into cider? Basque wines, sherries and vermouths do the trick.

■ 300 Florida Ave. NW (at 3rd St.)
METRO: Shaw-Howard U
PHONE: 202-986-3795 — **WEB:** www.anxodc.com
■ Dinner Tue – Sun

PRICE: $$

BAD SAINT

FILIPINO

MAP: 2-C2

With its teeny-tiny interior and notoriously long lines, you'll need the patience of a saint to secure a meal here—and it will be well worth the wait. Inside, an abundance of wood lends a tropical, Southeast Asian look, while backless stools, an open kitchen, and pulsating music deliver proof that Bad Saint is a young person's game.

Chinese and Spanish influences ensure that the Filipino cuisine here is creative and bold. Menu highlights include *ginisang ampalaya*, a plateful of stir-fried bitter melon tossed with salty and creamy black beans, and *kinilaw*, a Filipino take on ceviche. Covered with thick coconut cream, sliced crisp radish, juicy grapefruit segments, and puffed rice, the cubes of silky mackerel practically burst with bright flavor.

3226 11th St. NW (bet. Kenyon & Lamont Sts.)
PHONE: n/a
WEB: www.badsaintdc.com
Dinner Wed – Mon

PRICE: $$

BIDWELL

AMERICAN

MAP: 8-B1

You will indeed fare well at Bidwell. Tucked inside Union Market, it checks all of the boxes for a modern hot spot. Trendy, industrial-chic design (exposed air ducts, rough concrete walls) in the up-and-coming NoMa hood? Yes. Hipster-packed bar? Got it. Buzzworthy food? Indeed. Bidwell takes the farm-to-table trend and tops it—quite literally—since the rooftop garden supplies much of the kitchen's produce.

The menu may read classic, but this chef is no simpleton. Calamari stuffed with shrimp, spicy chorizo and served over piquillo pepper purée really goes for the gusto. Herb-roasted chicken is seared to a golden-brown, crispy delight, and when paired with heartbreakingly tender braised kale and crunchy, salty potatoes, it's positively perfect.

1309 5th St. NE (in Union Market)
METRO: NoMa-Gallaudet U
PHONE: 202-547-0172 — **WEB:** www.bidwelldc.com
Lunch & dinner Tue – Sun

PRICE: $$

BLACKSALT

SEAFOOD

XX 🍽

Fried, wood-grilled, simmered, steamed, or raw. No, it's not a line from *Forrest Gump*. As long as it swims, you can have it any way you want it at BlackSalt. It's all fish, all the time at this fish market-cum-restaurant in Palisades. There is a lively, bistro vibe here, where the bar is made for a cocktail and a platter of freshly shucked oysters while private booths appeal to a sophisticated, older crowd.

The concise menu trawls coast to continent for inspiration with dishes such as fried Ipswich clams and fish tacos to Provençal stew. Bigeye tuna tartare is silky; and potato-crusted skate wing is topped with a fragrant brown butter-mustard vinaigrette.

Hit the market on the way out for gourmet items to stock the pantry and soups to fill the freezer.

■ 4883 MacArthur Blvd. (bet. U & V Sts.)
PHONE: 202-342-9101
WEB: www.blacksaltrestaurant.com
■ Lunch & dinner daily

PRICE: $$

BLUE DUCK TAVERN ✿

AMERICAN

🍴 ♿ 🚰 🛏 🍸 🍷 📦

MAP: 1-A2

Simply put, Blue Duck Tavern will have you at hello. Set within the Park Hyatt, this upscale American tavern makes a dazzling first impression with its 25-foot entry doors, floor-to-ceiling windows, walnut wood seating, and highly coveted glass-enclosed booths. (And if that doesn't have you swooning, the dessert station, piled high with tempting treats, certainly will.) Whether seated in the plush dining room or expansive lounge—which features a totally separate cheese and charcuterie-focused menu—the gorgeous space and its well-to-do crowd are the epitome of casual sophistication.

At the center of the massive open kitchen sits a wood-burning oven, a behemoth centerpiece that turns out everything from fragrant, crusty bread to oven-fired Kansas Prime steak with Worcestershire gastrique. The menu spotlights such East Coast delicacies as cider-braised lamb shank from Shenandoah, VA; roasted duck breast from Hudson Valley, NY; and brown-butter roasted grouper from Florida.

In a unique twist, all of the dishes—from perfectly cooked Maine scallops with a mild horseradish jus to pan-roasted rock fish with spot-on dirty rice—are served not on plates, but in top-notch cookware.

■ 1201 24th St. NW (bet. M & N Sts.)
METRO: Foggy Bottom-GWU
PHONE: 202-419-6755 — **WEB:** www.blueducktavern.com
■ Lunch & dinner daily

PRICE: $$$

BOMBAY CLUB

INDIAN

XX   MAP: 1-C4

A fixture on the DC scene since Bush senior was in office, this Penn Quarter stalwart, owned by the affable Ashok Bajaj, still functions as a club for politicians and Beltway insiders. Polished and sophisticated with just a hint of spice, Bombay Club's environs are decidedly grown-up and the service appropriately white-glove.

If you can take your eyes off the senator snuggled into the half-moon banquette, the elegant Indian food doesn't disappoint. Tender, velvety squid is marked by a wildly flavorful combination of fennel and anise that dances on the tongue. *Saag gosht's* rich mustard greens and well-spiced lamb are a pleasant surprise, while the *gulab jamun*, milk dumplings with rose syrup and cardamom ice cream, makes a light and balanced finish.

■ 815 Connecticut Ave. NW (bet. H & I Sts.)
METRO: Farragut West
PHONE: 202-659-3727 — **WEB:** www.bombayclubdc.com
■ Lunch Sun – Fri   Dinner nightly   **PRICE: $$$**

BOQUERIA 😊

SPANISH

XX 🏠 🛋   MAP: 1-B2

Boqueria may be an import from New York City, but the flavor is straight up Spain. This slightly creaky row home belies the stylish and modern interior. Head upstairs for a tête-à-tête, while the main level's bar displaying meats and cheeses whets the appetite for what's to come. And what is to come? Tapas, tapas, and more tapas. Sure, there are salads and sandwiches, but with all-day small plates tempting you, why diverge?

The offerings are familiar, with plenty of Spanish classics (*croquetas*, those fried fritters of gooey deliciousness, for one), but contemporary creations make their mark. Colorado lamb meatballs in a rich tomato sauce with sheep's milk cheese are spot on, while *pulpo a la plancha* over olive oil-mashed potatoes delivers a pop of flavor.

■ 1837 M St. NW (at 19th St.)
METRO: Farragut North
PHONE: 202-558-9545 — **WEB:** www.boquerianyc.com
■ Lunch & dinner daily   **PRICE: $$**

BOURBON STEAK

STEAKHOUSE

XX &. 88 🖇 🖵   MAP: 7-C2

It's snuggled inside the sophisticated Four Seasons, so expect a moneyed crowd of executives and deep-pocketed locals who come here to dine on pricey dry aged and grass fed steaks and burgers. This Michael Mina steakhouse nails the modern masculine demeanor with its earth-toned palette and chocolate leather-inlaid tables. At lunch, the vibe is all business, while nighttime brings a scene-y crowd with a trendier take.

Dig right into the fresh-from-the-oven rolls while pondering their various cuts of meat. There are a few concessions (Korean barbecue salmon burger, anyone?), but it's really all about the cow. Duck-fat fries accessorize nicely, but the kitchen saves the best for last. Smoked s'mores are a creative rejiggering of the campsite favorite.

■ 2800 Pennsylvania Ave. NW (bet. 28th & 29th Sts.)
METRO: Foggy Bottom- GWU
PHONE: 202-944-2026 — **WEB:** www.bourbonsteakdc.com
■ Lunch Mon – Fri   Dinner nightly   **PRICE: $$$$**

CAVA MEZZE

GREEK

X 🛏   MAP: 4-C2

It turns out that you can be all things to all people, at least at Cava Mezze. This place manages to lure the post-work crowd who come to down drinks and talk shop; yet this casual Greek restaurant with palatable prices is also popular among families with young children.

There is a long list of shareable plates, plus seafood, meat and pasta. Additionally, quality ingredients sourced from area farms enhance simple preparations. While most of these honor the Greek standards (for instance, spanakopita is revved up by thick, creamy Greek yogurt and tender, buttery lamb chops are accompanied by fluffy fries), the kitchen also challenges convention. If that's not enough, it even delivers a few Med-influenced riffs—perhaps lamb sliders and orzo mac n cheese?

■ 527 8th St. SE (bet. E & G Sts.)
METRO: Eastern Market
PHONE: 202-543-9090 — **WEB:** www.cavamezze.com
■ Lunch Tue – Sun   Dinner nightly   **PRICE: $$**

CHERCHER 😊

ETHIOPIAN

�

MAP: 3-A1

There are some restaurants that feed more than just an appetite and Chercher is one of them. Set on the second floor of a townhouse just outside Little Ethiopia, this tidy jewel may have the bright walls and exposed brick so often seen in mom-and-pop spots, but rest assured that it delivers more than just a spicy stew with a home-kitchen feel.

Expect authentic items native to the culturally rich region of the Chercher Mountains. Rip off a piece of the cool and lacy *injera* and then dig into the lamb *wat*, a tender stew fueled by the fiery notes of berbere. Simmered vegetables add a welcome dose of earthy flavor on the side, but wait, what's that over there? It's the under-the-radar and off-the-menu dishes that lure expats with bated breath.

■ 1334 Ninth St. NW (bet. N & O Sts.)
METRO: Mt Vernon Sq
PHONE: 202-299-9703 — **WEB:** www.chercherrestaurant.com
■ Lunch & dinner daily   **PRICE:** ⊜

CHINA CHILCANO 😊

PERUVIAN

✗✗ ♿ 🍴 🍸 🖐 🖥

MAP: 3-B4

Bring a pile of friends and keep the piscos coming at this José Andrés hot spot, where a vibrant décor and bold, flavorful cuisine is the antidote to humdrum. China Chilcano is playfulness personified, even in the restrooms, where guests scribble on the chalkboard-painted walls.

Chinese-style steamed dumplings with *rocoto* chile-accented dipping sauce or hamachi served in a pool of slightly spicy *aji amarillo leche de tigre* reflect Peru's strong Chinese and Japanese cultural influences. *Causa limena* is layer after delicious layer of classic Peruvian flavors, albeit in an elegantly plated presentation. The *aji rocoto* sauce has a distinctly fruity essence blended with a garlicky goodness that makes everything it touches turn to gold.

■ 416 7th St. NW (bet. D & E Sts.)
METRO: Archives
PHONE: 202-783-0941 — **WEB:** www.chinachilcano.com
■ Lunch & dinner daily   **PRICE:** $$

CONOSCI

SEAFOOD

✗   MAP: 3-C2

Safely ensconced inside big sister restaurant Alta Strada (there's no other entrance), Conosci feels a bit like taking a girl on a date and having her older brother tag along. Yet, this hidden gem feels like a true find once inside.

The 30-seat room blends urban-chic (black ceilings and distressed metal wallpaper) with soft touches (votives and chandeliers). Plush blue couches or leather chairs anchor the bare tables and the marble bar is just right for solo diners who wish to interact with chefs. And even the unique raw fish-driven menu offers high-quality seafood that won't let you down. Imagine tender Japanese octopus or a plate of creamy risotto topped with local and deliciously sweet crabmeat—the Japanese-Italian mashup works wonders.

465 K St. NW (bet. 4th & 5th Sts.)
METRO: Mt Vernon Sq
PHONE: 202-629-4662 — **WEB:** www.conoscidc.com
Dinner Tue – Sat
                                                  PRICE: $$

CONVIVIAL

FRENCH

✗✗ 🛋   MAP: 3-B1

Truth be told, Convivial excels in all areas. It scores major points for its location, anchoring the base of City Market at O in the up-and-coming Shaw neighborhood; ranks high on style with its clean, rustic-modern aesthetic; and boasts service so downright relaxed, the servers wear jeans and sneakers. But the reason customers keep coming back to this lively and energetic hot spot is most certainly for the food: bold and playful takes on the tried-and-true that are made for sharing.

Popular with young professionals, families, and academics from nearby Howard, the whimsical, new-meets-old menu marries French and American cuisine—think garlicky, deep-fried escargots in a blanket, fried chicken coq au vin, or Chesapeake blue catfish bouillabaisse.

801 O St. NW (bet. 8th & 9th Sts.)
METRO: Mt Vernon Sq
PHONE: 202-525-2870 — **WEB:** www.convivialdc.com
Lunch Sat – Sun   Dinner nightly
                                                  PRICE: $$

THE DABNEY ❀

AMERICAN

🍴 ♿ 🚃 🍸

Your mother warned you about walking down dark alleys, but shush her voice in your head and traipse down Blagden Alley to The Dabney. It's like finding the end of the rainbow—make your way inside to discover a chic farmhouse-style interior, boasting an open kitchen, wood-fired oven, as well as a young, eclectic and well-dressed crowd. And then there is the food, which is nothing short of stellar.

In fact, Chef Jeremiah Langhorne—who interned at Noma and cooked at McCrady's in Charleston—is the patriarch here. As if that weren't enough, this Virginia native is the king of mid-Atlantic fish, local dairy, creamy grits, and other classic American ingredients.

This chef-driven menu is a successful marriage of traditional and contemporary flavors. If the likes of pan-fried Chesapeake catfish, dressed up with a mildly spicy hot sauce and served with calypso beans, bacon, wilted spinach, and brown butter foam ring a bell, then you're starting to get the picture. Then, flame-kissed from the grill and garnished with fried shallot rings, soy, and chili, grilled bok choy is far from a side dish. A buttermilk pie crowned with strawberry jam and yogurt foam makes for a divine finish.

🔲 122 Blagden Alley NW (bet. M & N Sts.)
METRO: Mt Vernon Sq
PHONE: 202-450-1015 — **WEB:** www.thedabney.com
🔲 Dinner Tue – Sun

PRICE: $$

DAIKAYA

JAPANESE

✗ ♿

MAP: 3-B3

There are restaurants where soaking in the atmosphere is part of the overall experience, and then there's Daikaya. This tiny, no-reservations ramen shop is always bursting at the seams (though the *izakaya* upstairs is an acceptable consolation prize if the wait downstairs is interminable). The unfussy space is filled with communal tables and a few booths, but the counter offers an unbeatable view of the steaming pots and hustle and bustle.

Pounding pop and rap music set the tone here, where you're expected to order, slurp quickly, and move on. There are just five types of ramen: *shio, shoyu, mugi*-miso (barley miso), spicy miso, and vegetable (100% vegan), but the bowls can also be customized—slightly—with the addition of extra toppings or extra noodles. If you want chicken-based ramen, check out nearby sib Bantam King.

■ 705 6th St. NW (at G St.)
METRO: Gallery Pl-Chinatown
PHONE: 202-589-1600 — **WEB:** www.daikaya.com
■ Lunch & dinner daily

PRICE: ⊜

DAS 👁

ETHIOPIAN

✗✗ 🍽

MAP: 7-C2

Nestled inside a classic Georgetown townhouse, Das is a haven of soothing colors and lush fabrics. Great care has gone into its styling, and the warm, generous spirit of the staff ensures that the entire experience is every bit as pleasant and refined.

The impressive menu runs the gamut from traditional Ethiopian cuisine to dishes that have the potential to take even the most seasoned and ambitious palate by surprise. A basket filled with *injera*—a spongy and sour bread that serves as both chaser and utensil—is never-ending. For a meal that won't disappoint, order the chicken and beef combination sampler. Then use rolls of that delicious *injera* to dig into mouthful after flavorful mouthful of surprisingly varied textures and degrees of heat.

■ 1201 28th St. NW (at M St.)
METRO: Foggy Bottom-GWU
PHONE: 202-333-4710 — **WEB:** www.dasethiopian.com
■ Lunch & dinner daily

PRICE: $$

DBGB KITCHEN AND BAR

MEDITERRANEAN
FRENCH

XX 🚻 🏠 🛋 🍸 🍺 🍳 🍽

DBGB Kitchen and Bar's City Center locale may rub shoulders with the likes of Hermès and Louis Vuitton, but this light-filled French restaurant maintains a relaxed elegance with tile floors, dark wood furnishings, and orb pendant lights. It's the kind of place where local politicos and dealmakers come to dish, drink, and dine.

The menu is varied, but you'll want to skip the ambitious Americanized cuisine and head straight for the house-made sausages and traditional French selections: pan-roasted salmon is well seasoned and crispy alongside an eye-pleasing vegetable assortment topped with crumbled bacon. Meanwhile, the flaky lemon tart, packed with thick lemon curd and accompanied by a quenelle of blood orange sorbet, makes for a truly satisfying finale.

■ 931 H St. NW (bet. 9th & 10th Sts.)
METRO: Gallery Pl-Chinatown
PHONE: 202-695-7660 — **WEB:** www.dbgb.com
■ Lunch & dinner daily   PRICE: $$

DECANTER

MEDITERRANEAN

XᵪX 🚻 🛋 🦞 🍳 🍽

MAP: 1-C3

Japanese-born Chef Gyo Santa has an impressive pedigree indeed. Trained at Le Cordon Bleu, Santa earned his stripes at Joël Robuchon's La Table before being lured stateside to the St. Regis in 2011. Decanter is the latest incarnation of the St. Regis' signature restaurant, and it reflects the traditional elegance of this Beaux Arts beauty while punctuating the space with a hint of contemporary panache.

In the kitchen, Santa presents a globally inspired menu prepared with confidence. Risotto ringed by meaty mushrooms and tinted green with arugula pesto is artfully plated, echoing the elegant background and setting an impressive tone. Then look forward to Moroccan-inspired spiced lamb that is tender, juicy, and tailed by rich, creamy macaroni and cheese further enhanced by bacon jam.

■ 923 16th St. NW (at K St.)
METRO: Farragut North
PHONE: 202-509-8000 — **WEB:** www.decanterdc.com
■ Lunch Mon – Fri   Dinner Tue – Sat   PRICE: $$$$

DEL CAMPO

LATIN AMERICAN

XX ఉ 🛏 🌰 🖥   MAP: 3-B2

Del Campo brings the spirit and style of *la estancia* to this burgeoning arts district, though you'll want to resist the urge to judge a book by its cover when visiting. Its rather bland façade belies a refined-rustic interior.

It's all smoke and meat at this Latin American steakhouse, where Chef Victor Albisu (who trained at Le Cordon Bleu in Paris) delivers straight-up South American flavor. *Asado* dominates the kitchen's cooking style, and the smoke imparts an intriguing complexity to everything—even the olive oil accompanied by pillowy *chapa* bread. Glistening cubes of tuna tartare are tucked inside a jar that swirls with smoke and is opened ceremoniously by a well-attired waiter, while the perfectly charred skirt steak is nothing less than butter-soft.

■ 777 I St. NW (bet. 7th & 9th Sts.)
METRO: Gallery Pl-Chinatown
PHONE: 202-289-7377 — **WEB:** www.delcampodc.com
■ Lunch & dinner daily   PRICE: $$$

DGS DELICATESSEN

DELI

X ఉ 🛏   MAP: 1-B2

DGS Delicatessen's corned beef, potato latkes, and braised brisket are so good that *bubbes* everywhere are crying into their matzo ball soup. Why trek to grandma's when DGS is right off Dupont Circle? White tile work, wood tabletops, and aluminum chairs lend a retro-but-updated look to this bright and airy restaurant that positively buzzes with a local business crowd.

Spoon up the salty goodness of smoked and cured fish before tucking into a never-fail deli sandwich. Thick, warm pastrami with a peppery crust and glistening with silky fat is layered on sliced rye for a simple, but oh-so-good meal. Shareable plates and heartier main courses (chicken schnitzel) have you swearing off that diet till tomorrow. Besides, aren't you too thin anyway?

■ 1317 Connecticut Ave. NW (bet. Dupont Cir. & N St.)
METRO: Dupont Circle
PHONE: 202-293-4400 — **WEB:** www.dgsdelicatessen.com
■ Lunch & dinner daily   PRICE: $$

THE DINER

AMERICAN

MAP: 2-A3

Nothing replaces a good diner. Where else can you tuck into a plate of bacon-wrapped meatloaf at 2:00 A.M.? The Diner is open 24/7 and its frenetic kitchen is always abuzz. Start off with a really good cup of Counter Culture coffee or if you're feeling more hair of the dog, a Bloody Mary.

It's not just standard diner fare here, where breakfast specials like bread pudding-French toast and tofu scramble with house-made salsa lean gourmet. Nursing a hangover? Straight-up comfort food is what they do best. Order the biscuit and gravy, with a flaky house-made biscuit slathered in creamy sauce with sweet Italian sausage—it's a decadent way to start the day. Finally, sip on a cookies-and-cream milkshake, best enjoyed atop a red vinyl stool at the counter.

■ 2453 18th St. NW (bet. Columbia & Belmont Rds.)
METRO: Woodley Park
PHONE: 202-232-8800 — **WEB:** www.dinerdc.com
■ Lunch & dinner daily   PRICE: 🐚

DISTRICT COMMONS

AMERICAN

MAP: 1-A3

Sometimes you want a place that crosses all of its t's without a lot of drama—and District Commons, set on a bright corner, hits the spot with its extensive drinks list, impressive beer selection, and comprehensive menu of eats. A U-shaped concrete bar dominates the scene, while wood-plank flooring, bare wood tables, and slanted concrete columns come together in a minimalist, slightly masculine look that's cool, comfortable, and broadly appealing.

The kitchen turns out American dishes, many with Southern influences, such as shrimp and grits or duck with sweet potato hash. Their strength is in the classics, so order one of the burgers, crispy hearth-baked flatbreads, or steamed mussels, before digging in to a slice of the fudgy Boston cream pie for dessert.

■ 2200 Pennsylvania Ave. NW (at Washington Circle)
METRO: Foggy Bottom-GWU
PHONE: 202-587-8277 — **WEB:** www.districtcommonsdc.com
■ Lunch & dinner daily   PRICE: $$

DOI MOI 👀

XX ♿ 🏠 ⊡   MAP: 2-B4

Set on a corner and flooded with sunshine, Doi Moi's interior is defined by its light, bright and mostly white modern look. Seating is limited to a long, expansive counter facing the exhibition kitchen as well as two dining areas with sleek tables framed by simple blonde wood chairs.

The restaurant's minimalist interior belies the flavor-packed riot of its food. The kitchen turns out spicy and bold Southeast Asian dishes, most with a heavy Thai bent. House-made Isaan-style pork sausage, salty-sweet and smoky in flavor, is expertly paired with pungent pickled vegetables and spicy chilies. Served in a deliciously spiced and creamy coconut curry, the *khao soi* braised chicken is fall-off-the-bone tender and placed atop toothsome egg noodles.

◼ 1800 14th St. NW (at S St.)
METRO: U St
PHONE: 202-733-5131 — **WEB:** www.doimoidc.com
◼ Dinner nightly   **PRICE: $$**

DUE SOUTH

SOUTHERN

XX ♿ 🏠 🍷 🍺   MAP: 4-A4

Set in the Lumber Shed building smack dab in the middle of the Yards Park, Due South is bright and airy with high ceilings and walls of windows, but the wraparound patio with its stellar views of the park and river is the place to be.

This kitchen's compass certainly points south and smoked meats are ever-present, but there's nothing simple about their prettied-up Southern-style cooking, enhanced with seasonal produce. Kale and heirloom tomatoes take the lead out of typically heavy shrimp and grits, while the Brunswick stew is particularly flavorful. If the hanger steak with broccoli rabe feels a little too—well, *northern*—take refuge in a slice of pie or cobbler. Beers by the draft or bottle are plentiful, but check the rotating list of specialty brews.

◼ 301 Water St. SE (at 3rd St.)
METRO: Navy Yard-Ballpark
PHONE: 202-479-4616 — **WEB:** www.duesouthdc.com
◼ Lunch & dinner daily   **PRICE: $$**

EATBAR

GASTROPUB

✕ ♿ 🍴 🎱 🍺   MAP: 4-C2

Where do you go when you want to throw back a few beers, listen to good tunes and catch up with pals? Eatbar. This casual spot is like your living room, only with better food (and a way-cool jukebox). It's all about the sharing economy here, where small plates rule the roost. The beer list is vast and the wine selection surprises with lesser known finds.

Small-batch charcuterie and whole animal butchery are passions of the chef, so the menu is meat-driven. But right sizing keeps portions in check. The carte is whimsically categorized so while "bready things" bring a summer tomato tartine with ricotta, "beasty things" unveil a Cotechino burger enriched with tomato aïoli and melted cheese. Seal the deal with "sweet things" like lemon-scented ricotta donuts.

■ 415 8th St. SE (bet. D & E Sts.)
METRO: Eastern Market
PHONE: 202-847-4827 — **WEB:** www.eat-bar.com
■ Lunch Sat – Sun   Dinner nightly   **PRICE: $$**

ESPITA MEZCALERIA

MEXICAN

✕ ♿ 🍴 🍹   MAP: 3-A1

The name is the first sign that this place takes its mezcal seriously. Step inside, where dark woods, concrete floors, and steel accents vibe industrial and you'll find shelves lined with the elixir. The selection is eye-popping and there are even certified Master mezcaliers on staff, so prepare to go in late tomorrow and kick back with a flight. That said, Espita Mezcaleria is so much more than just a watering hole.

The kitchen turns out tasty southern Mexican items—think tortas and tacos at lunch and seven types of house-made *mole* and other heartier entrées for dinner. Tender, shredded short rib-topped griddled *sopes* are moist and nutty, while the flaky grilled tilapia-packed tacos drizzled with a creamy chipotle-mayo are...one word...sensational.

■ 1250 9th St. NW (at N St.)
METRO: Mt Vernon Sq
PHONE: 202-621-9695 — **WEB:** www.espitadc.com
■ Lunch & dinner daily   **PRICE: $$**

ESTADIO

SPANISH

MAP: 1-D1

With its stone-accented walls, chunky wood furnishings, and poured concrete bar studded with Moorish tile, Estadio, or "stadium," plays up its Spanish influences. It's no surprise then that the focus is on tapas, but these unusual combinations and preparations offer a pleasant twist on tradition.

Golden-brown *jamón croquetas* are amped up with pickled cucumber; fava bean and almond spread is a thick and creamy snack; and sizzling squid a *la plancha* is drizzled with a citrusy salsa verde. Wash it all down with a glass of wine from Spain, Portugal, and the Canary Islands; a cocktail mixed with house-made tonics; or even a *slushito*—an icy blend of grapefruit, Bourbon, and amontillado, designed to counteract a hot summer's night.

1520 14th St. NW (at Church St.)
PHONE: 202-319-1404
WEB: www.estadio-dc.com
Lunch Fri – Sun   Dinner nightly   PRICE: $$

ETHIOPIC

ETHIOPIAN

MAP: 8-A3

With its large windows, bustling energy, and brightly hued interior, Ethiopic is an ideal fit for the melting pot that is H Street. Though minimalist, the dining room's bare tables are juxtaposed with pops of color from decorative wall hangings and other art.

This family-run spot turns out classic, well-made dishes with complex flavors, and the menu is a veritable treasure trove for vegetarians. *Tibs*, a marinated beef or lamb dish served with sautéed vegetables, delivers a kick of heat; while the slowly-simmered beef in the *sega key wot* proves that good things do come to those who wait. Of course, everything comes with the obligatory *injera*, thicker here than usual, and no meal is complete without a cup of that seriously rich Ethiopian coffee.

401 H St. NE (at 4th St.)
PHONE: 202-675-2066
WEB: www.ethiopicrestaurant.com
Lunch Fri – Sun   Dinner Tue – Sun   PRICE: $$

FIOLA ♣

XXX ♿ 🍽 ⛆ ✋ ♿

Polished and professional with an upscale setting made for brokering deals, Fiola is just what the politician ordered. Its central location near the Archives makes it a go-to for the power crowd, and the bar is perfect for blowing off steam after a busy day of debating.

Thanks to truly sophisticated cuisine, the somewhat stiff environs and overly scripted staff are soon forgiven—and despite its traditional feel, the menu actually allows for flexibility with the ability to craft your own prix fixe in addition to a tasting menu.

The chef's impressive cooking style is both ultra-luxurious and Italian-influenced, with a highly stylized bent to boot. Porcini cappuccino, a flan studded with foie gras, is proof positive that decadence reigns, while polenta with a foamy parmesan and gorgonzola *dolce fonduta* and black truffle is subtly elegant. Delicately prepared lobster wrapped in thin ravioli rests in a fragrant ginger- and chive-scented lobster nage; and chestnut-layered tiramisu topped with chestnut granita is a creative reboot.

As for the wine list? As one would expect, it's showy, littered with big names, and curated for those with sizeable expense accounts and companions to impress.

■ 601 Pennsylvania Ave. NW (entrance on Indiana Ave.)
METRO: Archives
PHONE: 202-628-2888 — **WEB:** www.fioladc.com
■ Lunch Mon – Fri   Dinner nightly   **PRICE: $$$$**

FIOLA MARE

SEAFOOD

MAP: 7-B3

Fact: Fiola Mare has a primo location. Resting right at the edge of the Potomac River, the setting hugs the river so every table comes with a view. It's part of the collection of restaurants run by Fabio Trabocchi, and like its name, this kitchen is seafood driven with Italian overtones.

Some dishes try too hard—the burrata has far too many competing flavors—but simple grilled seafood is always a good choice. Of course, there is no going wrong with dessert, specifically the chocolate soufflé crostata. While it may require a wait, your patience will be rewarded after one bite of the bittersweet Illanka chocolate *cremosa*, baked to order and fluffy-as-air with a toasted hazelnut crust. And though it needs no further gussying up, it is served with *torrone* gelato and truffle honey.

■ 3050 K St. NW, Ste. 101 (at 31st St.)
PHONE: 202-628-0065
WEB: www.fiolamaredc.com
■ Lunch Tue – Sun   Dinner nightly

PRICE: $$$

GARRISON

AMERICAN

MAP: 4-C2

Despite the heavy competition from its bustling Barracks Row location, Garrison stands apart with its farm-fresh food and its modern-rustic good looks. The brick patio, lined with flowering plants and herbs, makes a good first impression, and heat lamps extend the life of alfresco dining. Inside, abundant wood defines the look, which subscribes to the Scandinavian, less-is-more school of thought.

Area farms dictate the menu, but for hyper-seasonal selections, note the handwritten daily specials. The cooking style is ramped up American: smoke-infused potatoes are balanced by a pungent ramp aïoli; and green chickpea-crusted Chesapeake blue catfish is matched with a rhubarb coulis. Strawberry short cake parfait is like springtime in a glass.

■ 524 8th St. SE (bet. E & G Sts.)
METRO: Eastern Market
PHONE: 202-506-2445 — **WEB:** www.garrisondc.com
■ Lunch Sun   Dinner Tue – Sun

PRICE: $$

GHIBELLINA

ITALIAN

X & ⌂ ⟋

MAP: 1-D1

Ghibellina's marble bar is a favorite hangout, but don't let the cocktail-swilling patrons steer you away, since this kitchen gives its bar a serious run. Dark wood floors, iron accents, and exposed brick are a nod to the Old World, while the front sidewalk patio is a top people-watching spot.

Lunch is largely focused on salads and knockout pizzas. Ramp pizza reveals a delightful interplay between zingy, garlicky-onion ramps and creamy cheeses, including crumbled ricotta and *fior di latte*. Dinner expands to include antipasti, pastas (like *bucatini alle vongole*), and mains (like *pollo al mattone* or chicken under a brick). It's a linger-a-little-longer kind of place, so order dessert. The *affogato al caffe's* gelato with robust espresso is a nice finish.

■ 1610 14th St. NW (bet. Corcoran & Q Sts.)
METRO: U Street
PHONE: 202-803-2389 — **WEB:** www.ghibellina.com
■ Lunch Wed – Sun   Dinner nightly   **PRICE: $$**

HANK'S OYSTER BAR

SEAFOOD

X & ⌂ ⟋

MAP: 1-C1

The original of three locations, Hank's Oyster Bar promises a good time and full stomach. Snag a seat on the spacious front patio or take a table indoors where bottles of malt vinegar and Old Bay seasoning are a sign of things to come.

Meals begin with a bowl of humble goldfish cheese crackers, and then prepare yourself for a sea, *ahem*, of dishes. Feast on platters of raw bar beauties to bowls of steaming chowder to oysters any way you want 'em (Hog Island style involves dunking in a tangy lemon-garlic-tabasco-butter sauce, sprinkling with breadcrumbs and shredded cheese, and broiling until caramelized!). Of course, lobster rolls and crab cake sandwiches with Old Bay-seasoned fries are positively Proustian, conjuring up days at the beach from years past.

■ 1624 Q St. NW (bet. 16th & 17th Sts.)
METRO: Dupont Circle
PHONE: 202-462-4265 — **WEB:** www.hanksoysterbar.com
■ Lunch & dinner daily   **PRICE: $$**

INDIGO

INDIAN

🍴 🍹

MAP: 8-A2

It's yellow, not the telltale blue of its name, that defines this sunny Indian restaurant. Located in a cheerful yellow house with a patio full of colorful picnic tables, Indigo is far from fancy (it's largely self-service and food is served in disposable containers). But, how can you not adore a place where love notes from customers cover the walls?

Indian expats and residents line up for classic comfort food from the sub-continent, such as spicy chicken masala and melt-in-your-mouth-tender bone-in goat curry. Even side dishes are elevated here—*daal* is packed with smoky flavor and doused in a cardamom-scented sauce, while *paneer paratha* (flatbread stuffed with cheese, onion, chopped red chilies, and cilantro) is particularly fluffy and fantastic.

■ 243 K St. NE (at 3rd St.)
METRO: NoMa-Gallaudet U
PHONE: 202-544-4777 — **WEB:** www.indigowdc.com
■ Lunch Mon – Fri   Dinner Mon – Sat   **PRICE:** 🍢

INDIQUE

INDIAN

🍴🍴 ♿ 🍽 🍹

MAP: 6-C1

The name—no kidding—sure sums this spot up. Make your way inside only to discover that this bi-level beauté isn't afraid of making a splash with brightly painted walls hung with Indian art. Even the colorful cushions add a dose of serotonin.

The menu is equally inventive and plays both sides between classic and contemporary. Start things off right with samosa *chaat* featuring potato-and-pea samosas laid atop curried chickpeas and streaked with tamarind sauce as well as a zesty cilantro-chili chutney. Cooked in a tandoor, chicken *tikka makhani* is bathed in tomato- and caramelized-onion gravy, scented with fenugreek and ginger. The creative flair then extends to the bar, where drinks like a Mumbai Mule with rum, lime and curry leaf wet your whistle.

■ 3512-14 Connecticut Ave. NW (bet. Ordway & Porter Sts.)
METRO: Cleveland Park
PHONE: 202-244-6600 — **WEB:** www.indique.com
■ Lunch Fri – Sun   Dinner nightly   **PRICE:** $$

THE INN AT LITTLE WASHINGTON ✿ ✿

AMERICAN

XᵥᵥX 🍽 ♨ ♨

Nestled in a tiny Virginia town on the edge of Shenandoah National Park about 70 miles from the nation's capital, The Inn at Little Washington has long been the domain of Chef Patrick O'Connell and a destination in itself. The remote establishment began life as a garage built in the late 1890s, and has evolved since opening in 1978 into a culinary campus with guestrooms, a farmer's market, and shops.

This much-lauded Southern getaway was built for celebrating special occasions. More is more when it comes to the décor of these dining rooms—tapestries, tasseled silk lampshades, billowing fabrics, and floral patterns produce a riotous sense of opulence. Tables are elegantly set with the chef's personal collection of implements, some of which he has designed himself.

Guests choose from three tasting menus highlighting American cuisine often prepared using local product pulled from the restaurant's own gardens. Chilled veal tongue arrives with pickled vegetables and horseradish and mustard ice cream; while fried soft-shell crabs are sauced with orange and ginger. A perfectly seared duck breast gets a drizzle of brandied cherries plucked from the on-site orchard.

■ 309 Middle St. (Washington, VA)
PHONE: 540-675-3800
WEB: www.theinnatlittlewashington.com
■ Dinner Wed – Mon   PRICE: $$$$

IRON GATE

MEDITERRANEAN

MAP: 1-C2

Tucked inside the former stables and carriageway of an historic townhouse, Iron Gate is blessed with one of the city's most charming atmospheres. The cozy dining room is complete with requisite dark wood beams, exposed brick walls, tufted leather banquettes, plus that historic cherry on top: the roaring fireplace. The trellised garden patio, heated and open most of the year, is a close second.

The kitchen features a prix-fixe dinner menu along with small plates, where the chef displays myriad riffs on Greek, Italian, and Mediterranean classics. Chilled spring pea soup is refreshing and delicate; green tomato *keftedes* are a vegetarian version of the traditional Greek meatballs; and crispy arancini stuffed with spinach risotto hint at spanakopita.

■ 1734 N St. NW (bet. 17th & 18th Sts.)
METRO: Dupont Circle
PHONE: 202-524-5202 — **WEB:** www.irongaterestaurantdc.com
■ Lunch Tue – Sun   Dinner nightly   **PRICE: $$$**

IZAKAYA SEKI

JAPANESE

MAP: 2-C4

Set within a two-level townhouse in a residential area, Izakaya Seki delivers a simple, yet spot-on experience. With just 40 seats and a no-reservation policy, you may have to wait for your seat—either at the sushi bar on the first floor, or upstairs where exposed beams and shelves lined with sake bottles make for a Kyoto-chic ambience.

The father-daughter team ventures beyond sushi and sashimi to impress diners with authentic Japanese dishes, and it is evident the chef loves what he does. *Ojiya* soba, lovingly prepared in Japan and dried outdoors for one year before being stirred into the dashi and topped with sweet, flavorful pork belly, is nothing if not memorable. And delicate baby octopus braised in sake and mirin is sweet, salty, and just a bit smoky.

■ 1117 V St. NW (bet. 11th & 12th Sts.)
METRO: U St
PHONE: 202-588-5841 — **WEB:** www.sekidc.com
■ Dinner Wed – Mon   **PRICE: $$**

JACK ROSE DINING SALOON

AMERICAN

XX 🍴 🍸   MAP: 2-A4

What can brown do for you? If you're Jack Rose, a whole lot. Brown liquor is revered here, where four walls are lined with shelves of the stuff. There are 2500 bottles and there is even a library-style, rolling wall-mounted ladder to access it. Don't worry if your head spins before you take a sip; a Scotch specialist on the premises is happy to offer advice.

Jack Rose isn't just about the bar; the kitchen delivers a hit list of gastropub-style eats. Dandelion greens pesto atop chewy fettucine is creative and flavorful; fried quail served over toast and spread with creamy sawmill gravy studded with sausage crumbles is positively delicious; and a warm mini butter cake topped with a scoop of butter-pecan ice cream is as tasty as it is adorable.

■ 2007 18th St. NW (bet. California & Vernon Sts.)
METRO: U St
PHONE: 202-588-7388 — **WEB:** www.jackrosediningsaloon.com
■ Dinner nightly   PRICE: $$

JALEO 😊

SPANISH

XX ♿ 🚍   MAP: 3-B4

José Andrés's whimsical tapas take center stage at this outpost of Jaleo, one of three in the metro area. Sure, it has been open for over two decades, but there are no cobwebs in need of a dusting here. Creative, edgy, and irreverent, these are not your papa's tapas. *Croquetas de pollo* are crisped to a golden-brown and stuffed with ground chicken and béchamel, then served in a resin reproduction of a Converse Chuck Taylor sneaker for a unique and amusing presentation.

DC denizens can even get a taste of El Bulli's trademark science experiment-style of cooking since Andrés and Ferran Adrià were childhood chums and Andrés spent time at El Bulli. To that end, be sure to sample Adrià's liquid olives, which make for a delicious conversation starter.

■ 480 7th St. NW (at E St.)
METRO: Gallery Pl-Chinatown
PHONE: 202-628-7949 — **WEB:** www.jaleo.com
■ Lunch & dinner daily   PRICE: $$

KAFE LEOPOLD

AUSTRIAN

✗✗ 🏠 🍽️   MAP: 7-A2

Kafe Leopold (+ Konditorei) is the antidote to the too-cute-for-words pastry shop. Sure, there may be 26 different desserts to tempt your sweet tooth here, but there's nothing twee about this sleek space tucked in an alley behind posh M Street. Descend the stairs and discover a lovely courtyard garden—complete with a trickling fountain—before stepping inside to a relaxed arena with eye-catching photos and a decidedly modern atmosphere.

Savory choices include *rostbraten vom Angusrind* and *bratwurst*, but even with their delicious homemade taste, it's the final course that is first priority. Peruse the long list of *Kaffeespezialitäten*, and then nibble on a slice of *esterhazy* (five-layer hazelnut cake), a delicious éclair, or any other can't-go-wrong treat.

◼ 3315 M St. NW
PHONE: 202-965-6005
WEB: www.kafeleopolds.com
◼ Lunch & dinner daily   PRICE: $$

KAPNOS

GREEK

✗✗ ♿ 🏠 🍽️ 🍸 🍽️ 🏋️   MAP: 2-B3

From the exhibition kitchen with luscious meats rotating languorously on wood-fired spits to the chandeliers crafted of wine glasses and bottles, Kapnos is a buzzy spot that lures Capitol Hill staffers and couples on date night.

It's not just good looks; the food—mostly Greek with mezze for sharing—is just as alluring. Wood-roasted octopus tentacles are charred on the outside and tender on the inside. Follow this up with flaky phyllo pies, which when stuffed with roasted duck, are nothing less than divine. Small plates are ideal for snacking, while items like whole spit-roasted chicken or salt-baked dorado are designed for family-style dining. To wash it all down, peruse the innovative cocktail list, or opt for a glass of kegged lemonade.

◼ 2201 14th St. NW (at W St.)
METRO: U St
PHONE: 202-234-5000 — **WEB**: www.kapnosdc.com
◼ Lunch Sat – Sun   Dinner nightly   PRICE: $$

KEREN

ETHIOPIAN

MAP: 2-A4

Go ahead and order breakfast all day long, since Keren keeps the morning meal front and center. However, before you go "whole hog" and order bacon and eggs, take a second look. Keren is a showpiece of Eritrean cuisine. This East African nation has retained the best of Italy, a once occupying force, with many Italian-influenced, pasta-centric dishes popping up on the menu. A loyal crowd alternates between watching soccer, debating Eritrean politics, and filling up on the sizable portions.

Ful, a staple breakfast dish comprised of fava beans, jalapeño, tomato, and onion, is a good place to start (there are six variations). Then opt for the "five Eritrean" dishes for a well-rounded, veg-focused combo that is so good it renders you unable to pick a favorite.

■ 1780 Florida Ave. NW (bet. 18th & U Sts.)
METRO: U St
PHONE: 202-265-5764
■ Lunch & dinner daily

PRICE: ⬤

KINSHIP ✿

CONTEMPORARY

XXX ♿ 🐝 🧼 💻

Kinship is much buzzed about, thanks in large part to Chef Eric Ziebold's pedigree (he cut his teeth working with Thomas Keller). Along with his wife and partner Célia Laurent, Ziebold delivers inspired cuisine to a devoted following replete with urbane gastronomes and locals.

The setting across from the convention center belies its style; the three-part space comprises a book-lined and fireplace-warmed lounge, intimate bar, and minimalist-chic dining room, all crafted by DC designer Darryl Carter.

The à la carte menu isn't just a laundry list of offerings; it's a peek inside the chef's heart and mind. While selections from the "Ingredients" and "Indulgence" categories need no explanation, "Craft" items honor tradition and "History" selections pay tribute to his sentimental favorites. Pick and choose from the different themes for a bespoke tasting menu of dishes such as turmeric braised celtuce; butter-poached Maine lobster set atop house-made caramelized brioche for a lobster French toast; and duck *ballotine* over celery root "tagliatelle" in a cognac sauce. For a salty thrill of a dessert, fudgy Valrhona Guanaja custard cake is paired with pecan-praline ice cream and a buttery streusel.

■ 1015 7th St. NW (bet. L St. & New York Ave.)
METRO: Mt Vernon Sq
PHONE: 202-737-7700 — **WEB:** www.kinshipdc.com
■ Dinner nightly   **PRICE: $$$**

KOMI

MEDITERRANEAN

✕✕ 🕸   MAP: 1-C1

Climb the stairs of a historic Dupont Circle townhouse to find a diminutive restaurant with a focus on drama. There are just 14 tables, and the low lighting and hushed ambience scream date-night.

Komi has a high-end approach to a rule familiar with all kindergartners: "You get what you get and you don't get upset." To that end, there is no menu; instead, waitstaff ferry a cavalcade of delicate (read tiny) bites to you. Enjoy half a dozen savory samples (foie gras with apple foam; salt-cured cod infused with hay smoke) before moving on to the likes of mascarpone-stuffed dates and pasta with cinnamon-scented guinea hen ragù. The small plates just keep coming, even through a multi-course dessert, and all are served with a trademark flourish.

■ 1509 17th St. NW (bet. P & Q Sts.)
METRO: Dupont Circle
PHONE: 202-332-9200 — **WEB:** www.komirestaurant.com
■ Dinner Tue – Sat   PRICE: $$$$

KYIRISAN 😀

FUSION

✕✕ ♿   MAP: 2-C4

The Ma family's heart and soul is in this Shaw gem. It's hip, yet family-friendly, and a mix of locals, tourists, and political suits pack this energetic space.

Rabbit rillettes sandwiched between fried green tomato-turnip cakes drizzled with salted plum *sriracha* and sesame-soy sauce show off Chef Tim Ma's trademark blend of French-tinged Asian-flavored cooking. Sous vide duck confit is a don't-miss, clear winner, where moist, tender duck is sweet, smoky, and salty; balanced by caramelized Brussels sprouts; and finally offset by a tangy apple cider gastrique. One word—yum! All good things must come to an end but definitely order the *matcha pavlova*, a matcha meringue served with black sesame-flavored whipped cream for a nutty, not-too-sweet finale.

■ 1924 8th St. NW (at Florida Ave.)
METRO: Shaw-Howard U
PHONE: 202-525-2383 — **WEB:** www.kyirisandc.com
■ Dinner nightly   PRICE: $$

LA CHAUMIÈRE

FRENCH

✗ ⛶

MAP: 7-C2

It may be located on a bustling Georgetown street lined with modern stores and coffee houses, but La Chaumière is as Old World as it gets—much to the delight of its loyal crowd of old-money regulars and movers and shakers. Adorned with antique farm tools, repurposed barn wood beams, and a roaring fireplace, the dining room is both charming and cozy.

Even if the interior doesn't have you at *bonjour*, the food—rustic and unpretentious bistro classics such as escargot, pike *quenelles*, and steak frites—will do the trick. House specials include the *boudin blanc*, pike dumplings, and tripe stew. Of course, cassoulet is yet another house fave. They've also managed to sneak in a few newcomers, like Maryland crab cakes, but find even these cleverly Frenchified.

■ 2813 M St. NW (bet. 28th & 29th Sts.)
PHONE: 202-338-1784
WEB: www.lachaumieredc.com
■ Lunch Mon – Fri   Dinner Mon – Sat

PRICE: $$

LAPIS 😋

AFGHAN

✗ ⛺ 🛋

MAP: 2-A3

Lapis-colored columns set against whitewashed walls set the tone for a restaurant that gleams like its namesake jewel. From the stunning Afghan rugs warming the floor to the sepia-toned heirloom photos on the walls, this place exudes warmth and charm, albeit in a highly stylish manner.

Husband-and-wife owners Zubair and Shamim Popal share the fragrant cuisine of their native Afghanistan. Light and fresh without the heavy-handed spicing of other regional cuisines, this food is a delicious discovery. Split pea soup may sound basic but here it is layered with thick goodness. And *chopawn* is the real deal—this trio of grilled-to-perfection lamb chops is served with sensational cardamom-scented rice and draws you in forkful after fluffy forkful.

■ 1847 Columbia Rd. NW (at Mintwood Pl.)
PHONE: 202-299-9630
WEB: www.lapisdc.com
■ Lunch Sat – Sun   Dinner nightly

PRICE: $$

LE CHAT NOIR

XX

Friendship Heights's residents are lucky indeed, as the perfect French bistro—Le Chat Noir—is nestled within their quaint neighborhood. This darling spot embodies the ideal "corner" bistro with its inviting and warm ambience and classic French cooking. It's not cutting edge, but with a panoply of French hits, who cares.

Pissaladière, typically prepared with a flatbread, is literally puffed up here with a flaky pastry topped with caramelized onion, *herbes de Provence*, anchovies, and green olives for Mediterranean flavor. Savor the terrific broth of the bouillabaisse before tucking into the *merguez aux lentilles*, two thin sausage links served with green lentils set atop a salad. Savory and sweet crêpes are a mainstay of this menu, and brunch is superb.

4907 Wisconsin Ave. NW (bet. Ellicott St. & Emery Pl.)
PHONE: 202-244-2044
WEB: www.lechatnoirrestaurant.com
Lunch & dinner daily   PRICE: $$

LE DIPLOMATE

XX   MAP: 1-D1

Stephen Starr takes on the nation's capital with Le Diplomate, his pitch-perfect rendition of a Rive Gauche bistro. From the shiny and large brass windows to the zinc bar and the mosaic-tiled floor, it is all *très Français*.

Bread lovers rejoice; there is a paean to the crusty stuff at the entrance, where *ficelle*-filled bags and assorted loaves and rounds are lovingly displayed. This is straightforward traditional bistro food at its best: steak tartare, *croque monsieur*, steak frites with sauce béarnaise, and out-of-this-world *moules-frites*. Steamed with Pernod and served *marinière*-style, the mussels would be succulent enough on their own, but toss in a handful of those crispy pommes frites as well as a basket of freshly sliced baguette, and *mon dieu*!

1601 14th St. NW (at Q St.)
METRO: U St
PHONE: 202-332-3333 — **WEB**: www.lediplomatedc.com
Lunch Sat – Sun   Dinner nightly   PRICE: $$

LITTLE SEROW

THAI

MAP: 1-C1

It's very black-and-white at Little Serow, a spot that's neither fancy nor fussy and a stickler for rules. For starters, there's no phone, so you can forget about reservations. The menu is fixed, and that means no changes (nope, not even for your lactose-free, gluten-free, pork-hating friend). Want more spice? Don't even try to tell them how to cook. Still interested? You'd better get in line, because the door opens promptly at 5:30 P.M.

Little Serow lures hipsters with Northern Thai cooking that isn't handcuffed to please the lowest common denominator, plus wine pairings that perfectly complement the bold flavors. Classic minced chicken *laap* is ratcheted up, while the crispy fried tofu's Thai chili-enhanced sauce knocks out with a one-two punch.

1511 17th St. NW (bet. P & Q Sts.)
METRO: Dupont Circle
PHONE: n/a — **WEB:** www.littleserow.com
Dinner Tue - Sat **PRICE: $$**

LUPO VERDE

ITALIAN

MAP: 2-B4

The neighborhood is hopping with a crowded, convivial vibe, and Lupo Verde dances to that same beat. This two-storied restaurant has a bistro feel to its downstairs level, where a Carrara marble bar and communal wood tables welcome diners. Upstairs, the dining room has a low-key but quintessential luxe Italian look.

The kitchen too boasts some unique offerings—a roasted onion stuffed with four-cheese fondue is delicious, but it's really all about the homemade pasta and spot-on *affettati* here. The spaghetti is gloriously thick and chewy, while the charcuterie boards are crammed with delicious imported *salumi*, cheeses, olives, and *giardiniera*. Finish with a classic *affogato*, in which a shot of hot espresso is poured over a dollop of creamy vanilla ice cream.

1401 T St. NW (at 14th St.)
METRO: U St
PHONE: 202-827-4752 — **WEB:** www.lupoverdedc.com
Lunch Sat - Sun Dinner nightly **PRICE: $$**

MAKETTO 👻

✕ 🍴 🍳   MAP: 8-C3

If the hip gods of food and shopping mated, Maketto would be their love child. This unique space is equal parts style emporium and full-fledged restaurant serving sophisticated all-day dining. It may be steps from gritty H Street, but Maketto doesn't have a trace of grunge.

Taiwanese and Cambodian recipes influence the kitchen's appetizing, yet unexpected, Asian cuisine. Coconut milk-scallop crudo is at once razor-thin and ebulliently flavorful; a Taiwanese fried oyster omelette packs an eggy, briny punch; and grilled fish with coconut *nam prik* will elicit envy from your neighboring tables. If you have friends in tow, tuck in to the bountiful *bao* platter and its host of fillers, including those salty-sweet, perfectly marinated slices of rib eye.

▇ 1351 H St. NE (bet. Linden Ct. & 14th St.)
PHONE: 202-838-9972
WEB: www.maketto1351.com
▇ Lunch daily   Dinner Mon – Sat   **PRICE: $$**

MAKOTO

✕✕   MAP: 5-B1

Makoto is a testament to the love between a father and son. The chef, who assumed the top spot when his father passed some years ago, is warm and generous with stories of his father's passion and sacrifice. This place isn't about trend and there is a palpable sense of honoring tradition, so make a reservation, dress up, and expect to shed your shoes at the door.

You won't find à la carte sushi here, but you will be rewarded with a litany of skillfully prepared dishes. Seared Turkish royal sea bass with grilled asparagus and sugar snap peas along with a roasted red pepper sauce displays a harmonious balance. And, pan-seared sea urchin with crispy rice cake, burnt nori, *kinome* leaf and sprinkled with green seaweed is named a signature for good reason.

▇ 4822 MacArthur Blvd. NW (bet. Reservoir Rd. & W St.)
PHONE: 202-298-6866
WEB: www.makotorestaurantdc.com
▇ Dinner Tue – Sat   **PRICE: $$$**

MANDU

KOREAN

X ᛤ ⚓

MAP: 2-A4

You don't come to Mandu with your high-maintenance fashionista friend. But, if you're seeking the real deal—authentic and delicious Korean food without a lot of fuss—it is just the place. Everything is made with love at this family-owned original, and the portions are generous (especially at brunch, which is also light on the wallet).

Stick to the stews—*dak jjim* or *soon doobu*, *yokge jang*, and *mandu guk*—before moving up to the more hearty *galbi* or *bulgogi*. *Kimchi jjigae* has a heady perfume of garlic, chilies, and onions that announces its presence right after leaving the semi-open kitchen. And the *kimchi bokum bap*, heaped into a deep stone bowl, has a sweet-spicy sauce and is flavored with just the right amount of *gochujang* to add color and extra oomph.

■ 1805 18th St. NW (bet. S & Swann Sts.)
METRO: Dupont Circle
PHONE: 202-588-1540 — **WEB:** www.mandudc.com
■ Lunch & dinner daily

PRICE: $$

MARCEL'S

FRENCH

XXX ♿ ⚓ 🎱 ⊡

MAP: 1-A3

Marcel's lures a who's who crowd to its elegantly understated dining room, but there's nothing uppity about the amiable and genuine staff, who expertly walk the tightrope between attentive and fussy. Patrons come to linger over French-influenced meals enjoyed over multiple courses.

Pan-seared foie gras atop duck confit and paired with *eau de vie*-soaked cherries, and grilled quail over a warm artichoke salad are certainly French inspired. Curried butternut squash soup with apple, black sesame, and toasted cashew or enoki mushroom-topped halibut over parsnip purée speak to an entirely different influence. The almond financier topped with sunflower ice cream may be overdressed with one too many flourishes, but with its buttery goodness, who cares?

■ 2401 Pennsylvania Ave. NW (bet. 24th & 25th Sts.)
METRO: Foggy Bottom-GWU
PHONE: 202-296-1166 — **WEB:** www.marcelsdc.com
■ Lunch Sun Dinner nightly

PRICE: $$$$

MASSERIA ✿

With its chic and seamless blend of indoor and outdoor space, Masseria is a clear departure from its rough-and-tumble neighborhood. The classic former warehouse—complete with the requisite exposed ducts, concrete floors, and brick walls—has been glammed up with a stainless steel exhibition kitchen, chrome and leather furnishings, pendant lights suspended from nautical rope, and an impressive glass-encased wine cellar.

It's all very relaxed, albeit in a well-dressed way, and the feel-good vibe extends to the staff, who clearly like working here as much as diners enjoy lingering over the multi-course meals.

The chef's Puglian heritage comes through in the menu, which features three to five courses, along with a nightly tasting menu. The kitchen hits all the right notes balancing trendy and serious. Begin with a cigar box filled with focaccia so sinfully delicious, you'll be tempted to scarf it all down—but don't. You'll want to save room for the spicy fish stew, a thing of beauty practically brimming with tripe and lobster, or house-made *maccheroni* with thick and gamey goat ragù. Even dessert strays far from the pack, showcasing beet ice cream instead of the classic tiramisu.

■ 1340 4th St. NE. (bet. Neal Pl. & Penn St.)
METRO: NoMa-Gallaudet U
PHONE: 202-608-1330 — **WEB:** www.masseria-dc.com
■ Dinner Tue – Sat

PRICE: $$$

MÉTIER

CONTEMPORARY

✗✗ ♿ 🍽 ⬡

MAP: 3-B2

Chef Eric Ziebold's tasting room is set under the same roof as sister-spot Kinship—in fact, it is housed underneath. Guests arrive into this salon with a working fireplace and cookbook-lined shelves, which provide a lovely entry point where one can order a cocktail and nibble on bites.

The moniker is defined as a person's area of expertise; and Métier is an ambitious work in progress where the menu reflects the chef's personal experiences. A luxe take on canapés may include falafel with yogurt or lobster roll éclair, while poached Alaskan halibut resting over coconut milk-infused rice is a perfectly cooked and buttery delight. A love for meat is distinct in lamb ribeye presented atop hay, paired with bell peppers, and prettied by an olive-and-oregano jus.

■ 1015 7th St. NW (bet. L St. & New York Ave.)
METRO: Mt Vernon Sq
PHONE: 202-737-7500 — **WEB:** www.metierdc.com
■ Dinner Tue – Sat

PRICE: $$$$

MINIBAR ❀❀

XX ♿ 🍸 🍹 ⛶   MAP: 3-B3

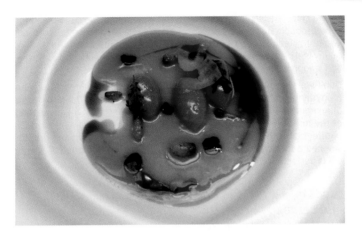

Set at the base of an antiseptic building are two frosted doors that mark the entrance to the mighty minibar. After a brief respite at their stylish lounge, be seated at a beautiful kitchen-facing counter. The focal point? A stainless steel workspace led by José Andrés himself. Then consider the fact that the chefs working these counters are as polished as the dishes themselves and know you're in for a veritable treat.

Track lights cast a bright glow upon each item and the bespoke crockery they arrive in. If crinkled metal or a drainpipe come to mind, you are starting to get the picture. And while dishes may be served simultaneously to seating groups, nary a detail is overlooked as each item is meticulously explained.

Certainly this is a culinary procession that is whimsical and innovative on every level. Here *pescadito frito* is actually fish-shaped seaweed crackers filled with *taramasalata*; while coconut cuttlefish stars cuttlefish slices that look like coconut and candied coconut that are in fact cuttlefish. Then, "This is Not Carrot Cake" is a mound of gingerbread soil with "carrots" made from sorbet growing out of it. Sound quirky? Indeed. But, it is also unique, fun and memorable.

■ 855 E St. NW (at 9th St.)
METRO: Gallery Pl-Chinatown
PHONE: 202-393-0812 — **WEB:** www.minibarbyjoseandres.com
■ Dinner Tue – Sat   **PRICE: $$$$**

MINTWOOD PLACE

AMERICAN

XX 🏠 🍷 🍸

MAP: 2-A3

Take a chic Parisian and a ten gallon-hat-wearing cowboy and blend for an improbable but oh-so-happy mix and you have Mintwood Place. This Western saloon-style space does Adams Morgan proud with its fun-loving, quirky feel defined by wood paneling, wrought-iron accents, and a rooster- and wagon wheel-enhanced décor.

Don't worry though as this melting pot of American and French cooking is anything but hokey. Snack on deviled eggs and pickled rhubarb before digging into escargot hushpuppies, a glorious Franco-American meeting of the minds. Starters like goat cheese and beet mountain pie or duck pâté entice with French finesse, while entrées like shrimp and grits or smoked pork ribs are stick-to-your-ribs, Southern-style good. Key lime pie is perfection.

■ 1813 Colombia Rd. NW (bet. Biltmore St. & Mintwood Pl.)
PHONE: 202-234-6732
WEB: www.mintwoodplace.com
■ Lunch Sat – Sun   Dinner nightly

PRICE: $$$

MOMOFUKU CCDC

ASIAN

XX ♿ 🚉

MAP: 3-A2

David Chang has come a long way since his tiny game-changing original in New York City's East Village. This impressive DC outpost is bright and shiny with multiple levels, lots of glass, and textbook-contemporary décor (think backless blonde wood stools).

Chang's signature street-style food is what put him on the map, and that's exactly what you'll find here. Those buzzed-about buns (let's face it, that's what you came for) are the stuff that pilgrimages are made of: pillowy soft, stuffed with meat or shrimp and slathered with tangy sauces. Rice cakes are yet another signature dish, while braised fried chicken is oh-so-good. Located just off the main dining room, the takeout Milk Bar carries desserts like the famed crack pie.

■ 1090 I St. NW (at New York Ave.)
METRO: McPherson Square
PHONE: 202-602-1832 — **WEB:** ccdc.momofuku.com
■ Lunch & dinner daily

PRICE: $$

NAZCA MOCHICA

PERUVIAN

XX 🍴 🛋 🍹   MAP: 1-C1

In a Peruvian version of upstairs-downstairs, this two-in-one restaurant comprises a *cebiche* and pisco bar downstairs with more traditional dining and a sleeker style up. Luckily, the fantastic *cebiches* are served both up and down. *Causitas* are the ultimate spud lover's comfort food and feature four towers of baked whipped potatoes topped with different flavors: caramelized fatty pork belly and onions; chicken salad dressed in mild *aji amarillo*; tuna *cebiche* with cilantro shoots; and slivered roasted piquillo peppers.

Kobe short ribs are glazed in a terrific, mildly spicy *aji panca*-honey, accompanied by yuca, potatoes, and *choclo* in a creamy *huancaina* sauce. In the end, sugar-dusted *alfajores* filled with dulce de leche round out the meal.

■ 1633 P St. NW (bet. 17th & 16th Sts.)
METRO: Dupont Circle
PHONE: 202-695-1249 — **WEB:** www.nazcamochica.com
■ Lunch Sun – Fri   Dinner nightly   **PRICE: $$**

OBELISK

ITALIAN

X   MAP: 1-B1

Obelisk attracts a surprisingly young, casual crowd for a spot that has been serving a fixed five-course menu five nights a week since 1987—a fact that's likely due to the restaurant's warm, neighborhood feel, even if the townhome it's set in could use a revamp.

The light and seasonal Italian cooking begins with a bang as an assortment of fantastic antipasti are quickly ushered to the table: creamy burrata; a sardine served over a tasty Prosecco-braised onion salad; crunchy puntarelle salad with a creamy anchovy dressing; and a thin slice of porchetta with a crisp shell and a rich, flavorful meaty center, to name a few. The second and third courses are overshadowed by the first, but the full experience is worth the two to three hours to enjoy.

■ 2029 P St. NW (bet. 20th & 21st Sts.)
METRO: Dupont Circle
PHONE: 202-872-1180 — **WEB:** www.obeliskdc.com
■ Dinner Tue – Sat   **PRICE: $$$**

OCOPA

PERUVIAN

XX 🏠 🛋

H Street's creative spirit spills over into Ocopa, which just so happens to sit across from the Atlas Performing Arts Center and Lang Theater. Dark wood walls could seem moody, but Peruvian decorations lighten the feel. And while there's an open kitchen, the place to be sipping a pisco sour is the massive "patio," complete with slanted roofing and red sails.

Inspiration hails from Peru, so expect a selection of ceviches, including daily specials, as well as small plates intended for sharing plus generously sized entrées. Share the *pollo* with your companions or order the *plancha de tierra*, which piles pork belly atop sausage atop chicken. And always leave room for the *arroz con pato*, a classic dish with duck leg confit, cilantro, rice, peppers, and peas.

■ 1324 H St. NE (bet. Linden Ct. & 13th Sts.)
PHONE: 202-396-1814
WEB: www.ocopa.kitchen.com
■ Lunch & dinner Tue – Sat

PRICE: $$

OLD GLORY BARBECUE

BARBECUE

XX 🏠 🍺

Though it skews more hipster than redneck, Old Glory Barbecue remains unpretentious all the same. Inside, it's all weathered wooden booths, worn stools, a bar studded with 1901 silver dollars, and rustic Americana décor, while upstairs is a popular patio that's heated during colder months.

Leave the white shirt at home since this succulent stuff will end up everywhere. Old Glory doesn't pick sides, so most regional styles are celebrated here with equal love and distinction. Stacked atop a potato roll, pulled pork is juicy and glistening with a tart and spicy sauce, while hearty beef ribs are slow-cooked for eight hours and fall-off-the-bone tender with a sweet-smoky flavor that has you gnawing like a dog on the bone.

■ 3139 M St. NW (bet. Wisconsin Ave. & 31st St.)
PHONE: 202-337-3406
WEB: www.oldglorybbq.com
■ Lunch & dinner daily

PRICE: $$

OSTERIA MORINI

ITALIAN

XX ⅄ 🛖 🛏

MAP: 4-A4

Yards Park is shaking things up along the Anacostia River, and Osteria Morini is among the high-profile restaurants headlining the riverfront rags-to-riches development. Thanks to its giant windows, abundant natural light, and open kitchen, this sleek and airy space truly shines.

One of several spinoffs of Michael White's original in New York's SoHo, the menu manages to be both impressive and familiar. Get the much-touted burger, which is celebrated at lunch and is also a nod to DC's less adventurous palates. Other items may also include wood-grilled meats, homemade pasta, and *polpettine in brodo*. Most impressive, however, is the generous bowl of *conchiglie* topped with pecorino *fonduta*, a culinary delight that screams "dig in" like nothing else.

◼ 301 Water St. SE (bet. 3rd & 4th Sts.)
METRO: Navy Yard-Ballpark
PHONE: 202-484-0660 — **WEB:** www.osteriamorini.com
◼ Lunch & dinner daily   **PRICE: $$$**

OTTOMAN TAVERNA 😮

TURKISH

XX ⅄ 🛖 📱 ⛶

MAP: 3-C2

This place is fit for a king. The interior is drop-dead gorgeous with a can't-stop-staring beauty. From its honeycomb patterns on the walls and that large mural of the Hagia Sophia, to its whitewashed walls with glimmering deep-blue pendants, this restaurant brings a little bit of Istanbul to the Mt. Vernon Triangle.

Sip a cool apple-rose tea while perusing the menu of Turkish cuisine infused with a modern bent. *Kirmizi mercimek corbasi* is a refreshing red lentil soup that starts things off right. Then dive into thinly sliced and delicious lamb and beef kebabs. But it's the moussaka, with its supple eggplant and potato slices and cinnamon-scented lamb, that must not be skipped. Freshly baked baklava or Noah's pudding end the meal on a syrupy note.

◼ 425 I St. NW (bet. 4th & 5th Sts.)
METRO: Gallery Pl-Chinatown
PHONE: 202-847-0395 — **WEB:** www.ottomantaverna.com
◼ Lunch & dinner daily   **PRICE: $$**

THE OVAL ROOM

CONTEMPORARY

XXX &. 🏠 🍽 🖥

MAP: 1-C4

The Oval Room has been the restaurant of choice for a particular brand of Beltway insider for over two decades, but like any doyenne worth her salt, this place underwent a recent nip and tuck to keep everything fresh. The dining room oozes sophistication with its plush carpeting and museum-style artwork. This elegance also extends outdoors to the chic sidewalk.

The food echoes the elegant environs with well-prepared classics, such as chicken liver mousse and nicely browned Amish roast chicken with crispy Brussels sprouts, wild mushrooms, sweet peas, fava beans, and shaved truffle. Other entrées such as shrimp and coconut grits with shellfish butter; or even molasses-glazed pork belly with cornbread purée show off a creative and Southern-inspired flair.

🔲 800 Connecticut Ave. NW (bet. 16th & 17th Sts.)
METRO: Farragut West
PHONE: 202-463-8700 — **WEB:** www.ovalroom.com
🔲 Lunch Mon – Fri   Dinner Mon – Sat   **PRICE: $$$**

OYAMEL 😀

MEXICAN

XX 🍷 🖥

MAP: 3-B4

Oyamel dishes out all the flavor of Mexico in a funky, festive space that delivers a quick hit of happiness. Snag a seat at the wraparound bar and guzzle thirst-quenching drinks while snacking on a parade of small plates, and you'll find that the rumors are true: José Andrés knows his stuff.

The kitchen's dedication to techniques and ingredients is clear, though the authentic south-of-the-border food far outshines the mediocre tacos. *Huevos enfrijolados* are a must order, crispy *chilaquiles* are spot on, and *gorditas* topped with Hudson Valley duck confit are nothing like their disagreeable Taco Bell cousins. The charred salsa is good enough to drink, with the perfect balance of acidity and flavor, and Andrés's take on *tres leches* offers a decadently sweet finish.

🔲 401 7th St. NW (bet. D & E Sts.)
METRO: Archives
PHONE: 202-628-1005 — **WEB:** www.oyamel.com
🔲 Lunch & dinner daily
                                    PRICE: $$

THE PARTISAN

GASTROPUB

XX ♿ 🛋 🍺   MAP: 3-B4

It shares space with sib Red Apron, a butcher shop and gourmet boutique, but The Partisan wins votes for its gastropub grub and hip feel. It is tall, dark, and handsome: picture industrial-height ceilings with exposed air ducts and a moody-broody color scheme.

Beer is big here, with 17 on draft arranged by flavor profile (tart/funky and fruit/spice are just two). At lunch, pick a meat (turkey breast, porchetta, or beef *döner*), then take your *tigelle* or flatbread, and smoosh it all together. At night, the menu steers offbeat and may include crawfish hushpuppies, beer-brined rotisserie duck, or smoked pork with mescal-baked beans. Charcuterie is also creative unveiling absinthe-lime rillettes, negroni-inspired Campari-rosemary salami, and curried pork pâté.

■ 709 D St. NW (bet. 7th & 8th Sts.)
METRO: Archives
PHONE: 202-524-5322 — **WEB:** www.thepartisandc.com
■ Lunch & dinner daily   **PRICE: $$**

PEARL DIVE OYSTER PALACE 👻

SOUTHERN

XX 🍴 🛋   MAP: 1-D1

With its slightly nautical ambience and casual pub vibe, this spot makes an ideal clubhouse for play-hard types. And while places that look this good usually don't have the menu to match, Pearl Dive's kitchen gives the dining room a run for its money.

The lineup is true-blue American food with a Southern slant, spotlighting starters like crawfish fritters, regional gumbos, and entrées like *Tchoupitoulas*—oyster confit with blue crab, Tasso ham as well as roasted corn. And then there are the incredible oysters, which are part of the Oyster Recovery Project (meaning you can feel good while you slurp them up with abandon). On your way out, make like the smug, in-the-know patrons and order the Brazos River-bottom pecan or rustic apple black iron pies to-go.

■ 1612 14th St. NW (bet. Q & Corcoran Sts.)
METRO: U St
PHONE: 202-319-1612 — **WEB:** www.pearldivedc.com
■ Lunch Fri – Sun   Dinner nightly   **PRICE: $$**

PINEAPPLE AND PEARLS ✿✿

CONTEMPORARY

✕✕ ♿ 🍴 🍸

MAP: 4-C2

What makes this such a memorable dining experience is that the food is ambitious yet playful, and completely devoid of formality or fuss. Whether you are served by the bartender or Chef Aaron Silverman, no one here seems self-important. Your continued enjoyment is paramount—an honorable feat considering that you are in for a meal that occupies most of your night.

The restaurant may be packed, but the ambience is pleasant and thoroughly comfortable. Know that the dining room's prix fixe includes wine pairing, but guests seated at the bar may choose to order drinks à la carte.

No matter where you sit, this cuisine is sure to spark interest. Highlights include a luxurious roasted potato ice cream, tangy with crème fraîche and topped with crisp potato threads, chives, and mouthwatering Osetra caviar. White asparagus wrapped in rice crêpe with mushroom duxelles and chicken mousseline may be inspired by *okonomiyaki*, but the result is pure innovation. This kitchen may save the best for last. Their towering chocolate soufflé's gentle bitterness is balanced with caramel-sweet honeycomb ice cream and nutty grains of toasted buckwheat for a dessert that is nothing short of perfect.

■ 715 8th St. SE (bet. G & I Sts.)
METRO: Eastern Market
PHONE: 202-595-7375 — **WEB:** www.pineappleandpearls.com
■ Dinner Tue-Fri
                                              PRICE: $$$$

PLUME ❀

EUROPEAN

XXXX ♿ 🐝 🍽 🖼

Gentlemen don a jacket and ladies grab those pearls because dinner at this dining room of The Jefferson Hotel is a very elegant affair. Walk past marble pillars, check-in at Plume's reception desk, and expect to be cordially escorted to your table in this sequestered lair.

Gilded and sparkling, the room's opulence pays homage to America's colonial grandeur with plush silk wallpaper depicting the grounds of Thomas Jefferson's Monticello. Large tables spread over checkerboard-tiled floors are laid with sumptuously starched linens, polished silver, and heavy crystal; while bright flowers pop against the room's aubergine-hued accents. A roaring fireplace is a cozy wintertime bonus.

This modern menu applies classic European technique to a bevy of local ingredients inspired by the seasons. The prix-fixe unveils an evening of gastronomic opportunity. Regulars know to commence with the Chesapeake Bay Blue Crab tea. This tableside preparation is a succulent distillation poured over myriad garnishes. King salmon slow-poached in hot beeswax is another showstopper; while a Pavlova with crystallized violets and strained yogurt proves this kitchen is solid from start to finish.

■ 1200 16th St. NW (at M St.)
METRO: Farragut North
PHONE: 202-448-2300 — **WEB:** www.plumedc.com
■ Dinner Tue – Sat   PRICE: $$$$

PROOF

AMERICAN

XX   ♿   ☂   ❀

MAP: 3-B3

It may be said that the proof is in the pudding, but this particular restaurant proves its mettle with wine. Inside, contemporary pendant lights, dark wood floors, and walls showcasing bottles of, yes, wine, have a chic and modern effect. The liquid is more than artwork, though, and oenophiles and newbies alike will find satisfying sips.

Proof's food reflects an international point of view—envision flaky and glistering flatbread topped with chickpeas, red onion, green olives, pickled radish, and a silky, smoked eggplant emulsion; or spicy chicken and pork meatballs paired with ricotta ravioli. If you manage to leave room for dessert, consider forgoing something sweet and instead sink your teeth into a selection from the comprehensive cheese list.

■ 775 G St. NW (at 8th St.)
METRO: Gallery Pl-Chinatown
PHONE: 202-737-7663 — **WEB:** www.proofdc.com
■ Lunch Tue – Fri   Dinner nightly   PRICE: $$

PURPLE PATCH

FILIPINO

XX   🛋

MAP: 2-B2

How do you pay tribute to the classics while simultaneously bumping them up ever so much? Just ask the Purple Patch. This restaurant delivers note-perfect Filipino food with just the right amount of playfulness. Case in point? The *adobo*-radicchio wraps, which take the familiar flavors of chicken in *adobo*, top it with pickled papaya, then surround it with the crunch of radicchio. Pork *sinigang* is considered a typical (read staple) dish, but is truly worthy of exaltation. Here, tender chunks of pork are bathed in a lemon broth that is so generously sized it seems indecent, and with potatoes, vegetables, and fluffy jasmine rice, it's plain sinful.

Even dessert is a thing of wonder. Purple yam ice cream? Who knew a tuber could be this magically delicious?

■ 3155 Mt Pleasant St. NW (bet. Kilbourne Pl. & Keyton St.)
METRO: Columbia Heights
PHONE: 202-299-0022 — **WEB:** www.purplepatchdc.com
■ Lunch Sat – Sun   Dinner nightly   PRICE: ⚥

RAPPAHANNOCK OYSTER BAR

SEAFOOD

MAP: 8-B1

Set inside the buzzing Union Market, Rappahannock Oyster Bar is oh-so-much *more* than a popular bivalve joint. The feel-good revival story behind it will make you feel more philanthropist than hungry diner, and the ambience is everything you'd expect and then some: counter space, communal seating, a sprinkling of outdoor tables, and an open-air vibe.

While the spotlight here is on the raw bar (order the sampler, a veritable love letter to the Virginia waters), the cooked dishes give those half-shells a run for their money. Clam chowder is thick, creamy, and full of briny meat, and though the steamed shrimp dish sounds simple, these shell-on specimens, served with a hunk of bread, sautéed onions, peppers, and spice, are a messy but delicious affair.

■ 1309 5th St. NE (in Union Market)
METRO: NoMa-Gallaudet U
PHONE: 202-544-4702 — **WEB:** www.rroysters.com
■ Lunch & dinner Tue – Sun   **PRICE: $$**

RASIKA

INDIAN

MAP: 3-B4

This ever-popular hot spot (reserve in advance) lures all types with its kitsch-free Indian cuisine and the kind of lively, low-key ambience that's as perfectly suited for a casual night out with friends as it is a formal dinner with colleagues or a festive celebration.

It's difficult to live up to the hype, but Rasika turns out several winning dishes. *Palak chaat's* crispy spinach leaves tossed with *raita*, sweet tamarind, and date chutneys bursts with flavor, and the tender, yet crunchy okra is a perfect marriage of spicy and sour. Match these with expertly prepared, house-made paneer skewered with peppers and onions and accompanied by tasty green chutney.

For those who can't get a table, Rasika has a second, less-trafficked location in the West End with a similar menu.

■ 633 D St. NW
PHONE: 202-637-1222
WEB: www.rasikarestaurant.com
■ Lunch Mon – Fri   Dinner Mon – Sat   **PRICE: $$$**

THE RED HEN 🐽

AMERICAN

✗   MAP: 2-D4

You can't miss this place—there's a giant red hen painted on the façade of the century-old building—but if you're a Bloomingdale resident, you're likely a regular already. The look is farmhouse funky complete with reclaimed timber, exposed brick, and a wood-burning oven in the kitchen, but don't let the country-cute appeal fool you: there's a CIA-trained chef manning the stove. It's largely American with an Italian bent, plus a few offbeat ingredients (*shichimi togarashi* and *za'atar*) thrown in for good measure.

Pasta is a sure thing, and the crowd favorite, mezze rigatoni with fennel sausage ragù, is proof positive that simple isn't boring. Caramelized scallops atop creamy polenta are delicious, but save room for the just-sweet-enough maple custard.

■ 1822 1st St. NW (at Seaton Pl.)
PHONE: 202-525-3021
WEB: www.theredhendc.com
■ Dinner nightly   PRICE: $$

RESTAURANT NORA

CONTEMPORARY

✗✗ 🥢 🍽   MAP: 1-A1

Committed food activist and Chef Nora Pouillon is the Alice Waters of DC, as her eponymous restaurant has been a champion of the farm-to-table movement long before it was a catch phrase.

The interior's whitewashed exposed brick walls, framed quilts, and beamed ceilings speak to a country chic sensibility, but nothing's more impressive than the ingredients gracing your plate. This is, after all, the first certified organic restaurant in the U.S.

The tasting menu with vegetarian options is definitely the way to go. Begin with a cold (beet salad with feta) or hot (chili-spiced calamari) small plate before diving in to a flavor-packed entrée, like the flaky cod in a ginger-cilantro emulsion with extra-sweet snow peas, tender bok choy, and crispy yams.

■ 2132 Florida Ave. (at R St.)
METRO: Dupont Circle
PHONE: 202-462-5143 — **WEB:** www.noras.com
■ Dinner Mon – Sat   PRICE: $$$

RIPPLE

AMERICAN

XX ♿ 🍴 📶 🚲   MAP: 6-C1

Warm and inviting with terrific food to boot, Cleveland Heights residents are lucky to call this perfect rendition of a local spot their own. Inside, a quirky hodgepodge of mirrors, quilt-patterned banquettes, and nickel-topped tables further enhance the welcoming vibe.

House-made charcuterie and a varied cheese selection set the tone for a menu that's homey with a dash of haute. Lamb tartare is topped with an olive-anchovy aïoli and served over rice (both fluffy and toasted for textural contrast), while the roasted lamb saddle with mint-pistachio "pesto" is expertly cooked. Ripple does comfort food right—there's an entire menu dedicated to different varieties of grilled cheese—and it goes without saying that brunch is a seriously big deal here.

■ 3417 Connecticut Ave. NW (bet. Macomb & Ordway Sts.)
METRO: Cleveland Park
PHONE: 202-244-7995 — **WEB:** www.rippledc.com
■ Lunch Sun   Dinner nightly   **PRICE: $$**

RIS

AMERICAN

XX ♿ 🍴 📶   MAP: 1-A3

Ris Lacoste helms the stove at this terrific neighborhood spot, a draw for diners in the company of family, business associates, and lovers alike. The sprawling, light-filled dining room is dressed in earth tones and filled with intimate corners for an air of seductive sophistication. And the menu, with its ramped-up takes on the tried-and-true, toes the line between familiar and surprising.

Loaded with butter and olive oil and jazzed up with red pepper flakes, linguine with clams is briny and delicious, and chicken Milanese has just the right amount of breading beneath its zippy tomato topping. Even the crown of cauliflower is interesting and complex, thanks to an ensemble of roasted vegetables slicked with mustard cream and an army of flavors.

■ 2275 L St. NW (at 23rd St.)
METRO: Foggy Bottom-GWU
PHONE: 202-730-2500 — **WEB:** www.risdc.com
■ Lunch Sun – Fri   Dinner nightly   **PRICE: $$**

ROOFERS UNION

AMERICAN

XX 🏠 � MAP: 2-A3

Roofers Union is fun, pure and simple. This bi-level gastropub zeroes in on drinks downstairs, while upstairs has an airy wall of windows and a focus on food. Either up or down, the mood is light and occasional live music adds to the convivial vibe.

The well-made pub grub is also well-rounded and the large menu has something for everyone—just one reason why it's packed with regulars. Asparagus salad starts things off in a refreshing manner, while fried chicken thighs with a honey-*sriracha* sandwich isn't so much a gamechanger as a downright tasty crowd-pleaser. Meat lovers rejoice in the sausage trio with its beer-poached bratwurst, veal heart sausage as well as an Italian version set on a bed of peppers, onions and melted provolone.

🔲 2446 18th St. NW (bet. Belmont & Columbia Rds.)
PHONE: 202-232-7663
WEB: www.roofersuniondc.com
🔲 Dinner nightly PRICE: $$

ROSE'S LUXURY ❀

CONTEMPORARY

XX 🛖 🍸 🎴

Despite its prime Capitol Hill location, there's nothing buttoned up about Rose's Luxury. This local fave's food and mood practically sings of funkier digs.

Tucked inside a row house, the cozy-yet-contemporary space is industrial-chic to a tee with bare plywood banquettes, concrete accents, and strings of lights. The youthful-cum-playful atmosphere is bolstered by a hipster-heavy crowd, who queue up early or outsource a placeholder in line for this no-reservations spot.

Innovative yet approachable, the food bobs and weaves with absolute precision. Its melting pot of flavors is dizzying at times, and every dish is far from forgettable. Choose from cool or warm small plates: charred carrots tempered by tart house-made yogurt with harissa for extra pizzazz; crispy, complex jerk spice-marinated fried pig's ears; or an intensely elaborate salad of pork sausage, habanero, peanuts, and lychee. Pasta is turned on its head with unorthodox blends like a tomato-y *penne alla vodka* pepped up with Thai basil. And while several family-style dishes are also on offer, the small plates are far more intriguing. To end the meal on a sweet note, dig into the befuddling—yet delicious—*Fernet* and cola tiramisu.

■ 717 8th St. SE (bet. G & I Sts.)
METRO: Eastern Market
PHONE: 202-580-8889 — **WEB:** www.rosesluxury.com
■ Dinner Mon – Sat   **PRICE: $$**

ROYAL

LATIN AMERICAN

✗✗ 🍽 🍹

MAP: 2-D4

They may not be regal, but there's a family behind Royal. The owner, along with his parents and sister, have a hand in this all-day dining spot designed for residents who want to eat well without breaking the bank. Budgets aside, Royal doesn't scrimp on style or flavor either. Tin-ceilings and other original touches were retained and the vibe is welcoming, yet casual (no reservations or hostess).

Golden-brown empanadas with paper-thin exteriors are stuffed with juicy pork for a taste of mama's Colombian kitchen and the *aji* sauce is can't-get-enough-of-it good. Chicken and sprouts sure sounds basic, but with tender grilled chicken drumsticks accompanied by roasted Brussels sprouts and charred scallions with a *chimi*-style white sauce, it's anything but boring.

■ 501 Florida Ave. NW (at 5th St.)
METRO: Shaw-Howard U
PHONE: 202-332-7777 — **WEB:** www.theroyaldc.com
■ Lunch & dinner daily

PRICE: $$

SAKURAMEN

JAPANESE

✗

MAP: 2-A3

Sometimes all you really want is a delicious meal in a comfortable setting. No fuss, no hipper-than-thou patrons, just good food. Sakuramen, in the basement of a row house in Adams Morgan, is on hand to soothe your soul with its wide variety of that steaming bowl of love—ramen.

In fact, it's all about these toothsome noodles here. *Gojiramen* is a traditional shoyu ramen, while *chosun* shows off a Korean influence with Angus *bulgogi* and kimchi. *Gyoza* and steamed buns are available for good measure. *Sakuramen* is naturally the house special and the kitchen changes things up with a vegetable broth made from mushrooms and seaweed. Braised bamboo shoots, portobello caps, and other vegetables bob amid the curly noodles for a perfectly satisfying meal.

■ 2441 18th St. (bet. Belmont & Columbia Rds.)
PHONE: 202-656-5285
WEB: www.sakuramen.info
■ Lunch Fri – Sun   Dinner Tue – Sun

PRICE: 🍜

1789

AMERICAN

ХХ 🦪 🥾 🍴

MAP: 7-A2

1789 is classic Georgetown—think wooden beams, American antiques, and flickering fireplaces all nestled inside a Federal-period townhouse on a quaint residential street. The restaurant's six dining rooms, each with their own layout and décor, are spread across three floors, while the basement houses The Tombs, a storied watering hole for university students.

The mood here is definitely special occasion, and the menu bows to that by sticking with what works: seasonal, carefully curated American fare that's simple and straightforward. Butternut squash soup topped with fried carrot is appropriately creamy; pork tenderloin is dressed up with a puffed pork *chicharrón* for a tasty garnish; and key lime soufflé is that perfect yin and yang of sweet and tart.

◼ 1226 36th St. NW (at Prospect St.)
PHONE: 202-965-1789
WEB: www.1789restaurant.com
◼ Dinner nightly   **PRICE: $$$**

SOI 38

THAI

ХХ 🏠

MAP: 1-A3

Sidewalk seating is plentiful, but step inside Soi 38 and you'll discover a delightfully modern and elegant dining room. Black walls are emblazoned with gold-painted images, making a dramatic first impression. While the look is upscale, the menu celebrates the street foods of Thailand, offering a blend of influences from the owners' native Bangkok and the chef's Northern Thai heritage.

Begin with *khao soi*, hailing from Chiang Mai and filled to the brim with a turmeric-yellow, dried chili, and coconut milk-rich curry bursting with chicken and noodles. *Kua kling* is a ground pork curry served with cucumber slices and crisp green beans over rice; while *seua rong hai* is that holy grail of expertly grilled flank steak coupled with a fiery and crunchy green papaya salad.

◼ 2101 L St. NW (entrance on 21st St.)
METRO: Farragut North
PHONE: 202-558-9215 — **WEB**: www.soi38dc.com
◼ Lunch & dinner daily   **PRICE: $$**

SONOMA

CONTEMPORARY

XX &. 🚪 🛏 🐝 ▭

MAP: 4-A1

This popular wine bar is just the spot to unwind after a long day on the Hill. Exposed brick walls and a polished wood-backed banquette are at once laid-back and luxe, while the sidewalk out front offers a breath of fresh air. Despite its name, Sonoma features an extensive global wine list, and by-the-glass offerings are numerous. Take a sip around the world with a flight like The Yellow Brick Road, which spotlights a trio of sauvignon blancs from Bordeaux, New Zealand, and Napa.

The impressive list of house-crafted charcuterie includes pork *rillettes*, *pâté de campagne*, gravlax, and chicken liver mousse. However, heartier appetites will meet their match with burgers, pizzas, and pasta, including gnocchi with an eggplant ragù akin to ratatouille.

■ 223 Pennsylvania Ave. SE (bet. Independence Ave. & 3rd St.)
METRO: Capitol South
PHONE: 202-544-8088 — **WEB:** www.sonomadc.com
■ Lunch Sun – Fri   Dinner nightly   **PRICE: $$**

SORRISO

ITALIAN

X 🚪

MAP: 6-C1

If you could get a PhD in pizza-making, it would be hanging on the wall of this Cleveland Park haunt. In fact, the owner's son Pietro did indeed study the art and science of crafting the perfect pizza at the Scuola Italiana Pizzaioli in Venice, and that higher learning certainly pays off in his 13-inch pies.

Baked in a wood-and-gas-fired oven with a hot stone base, the crust is chewy and smoky. Creamy mozzarella and tomato sauce serve as the most enticing fresh slate you've ever tasted, but top it with a dizzying array of meat and vegetables for more fun. There are also salads, house-made pastas, as well as a few Northern accented-entrées (maybe Venetian fish stew or *ossobuco di agnello*). But really, with pizza this good, why stray?

■ 3518 Connecticut Ave. NW (bet. Ordway & Porter Sts.)
METRO: Cleveland Park
PHONE: 202-537-4800 — **WEB:** www.sorrisoristorante.net
■ Dinner nightly   **PRICE: $$**

Culinary Agents

Connecting the industry

Find the best jobs. Find the best people.

CulinaryAgents.com

THE SOURCE BY WOLFGANG PUCK

ASIAN

✗✗ ⅙ 🛏 ✄ ♨ ⬭   MAP: 3-B4

Say what you want—this restaurant is, after all, located inside the Newseum, a place where free speech is revered—but Wolfgang Puck manages to churn out reliably good food in trademark chic settings, and the Source is certainly no exception to this rule.

The Pan-Asian bistro doesn't capture headlines with every plate, but there are some real scene stealers, especially the dim sum platter and its appetizing presentation of solidly prepared dumplings and a delicately crispy lobster roll. Wonton soup, largely overlooked elsewhere, is elevated to an art form here, where a porcelain tureen brimming with the signature 20-hour broth is wheeled tableside for individual ladling. Aromatic, rich, and complex, this version grabs attention from first slurp.

■ 575 Pennsylvania Ave. NW (at 6th St.)
METRO: Archives
PHONE: 202-637-6100 — **WEB:** www.wolfgangpuck.com
■ Lunch & dinner Mon – Sat   **PRICE: $$**

THE SOVEREIGN

BELGIAN

✗✗ 🛏 🍺   MAP: 7-B2

Tucked down a candlelit alley in Georgetown, The Sovereign takes the dark wood and high tables of the classic bar and warms it up with richly patterned fabrics, red leather chairs, and soft lighting. This place makes no bones about its allegiance to beer, proudly offering over 50 options on draft and more than 300 bottles.

Of course the kitchen celebrates Belgian cuisine as much as it does beer. Items include *bitterballen*, shrimp croquettes, *tartes flambeés*, and *carbonade flamande*—a beer-braised beef stew. It's also easy to see why a street treat like *gaufres liégoise* are elevated here thanks to the addition of pistachio paste-flavored whipped cream. But for the real deal, dive into steamed mussels accompanied by deliciously skinny frites.

■ 1206 Wisconsin Ave. NW (bet. M & Prospect Sts.)
PHONE: 202-774-5875
WEB: www.thesovereigndc.com
■ Lunch Sat – Sun   Dinner nightly   **PRICE: $$**

SUSHI OGAWA

JAPANESE

XX 🍴　　　　　　　　　　　　　　　MAP: 2-A4

Sushi Capitol's much-talked-about chef, Minoru Ogawa, now runs the show at this hot spot tucked inside a stunning art deco building in upscale Kalorama Heights. The décor is everything you'd expect from a chic Japanese restaurant: subtly textured walls, honey-hued wood, and minimalist details.

Sushi is front and center here and omakase is certainly the way to go, though an à la carte menu is offered at the handful of tables in the intimate dining room. The fish is from Japan by way of the New Fulton Fish Market in New York City, and some pieces dazzle more than others. Tender baby snapper, torched Japanese barracuda, sea eel paired with octopus and brushed with *unagi* sauce, and hiramasa with slivered *myoga* and grated ginger root are among the hits.

■ 2100 Connecticut Ave. NW (Kalorama Rd. & Wyoming Ave.)
METRO: Dupont Circle
PHONE: 202-813-9715 — **WEB:** www.sushiogawa.com
■ Dinner Mon – Sat　　　　　　　　　　　　**PRICE: $$$$**

SUSHI TARO ✿

✗✗   MAP: 1-C1

Sushi aficionados know to give this beloved Dupont Circle gem a pass for its odd location—adjacent to a large-chain pharmacy and accessed by a short flight of steps. However, the interior opens up into a comfortable and warmly attended dining room. Sushi Taro offers fine à la carte and numerous tasting menus, but the experience at the omakase counter is truly stellar.

Scoring a meal at the omakase counter proves challenging since seats can only be booked online, via e-mail, 30 days in advance. Once secured, a reservation at the counter grants entrée to a cloistered room where Chefs Nobu Yamazaki and Masaya Kitayama cater to a mere handful of diners.

Following the construct of kaiseki, the meal is a series of artistically composed courses such as grilled marinated tuna cheek or squid-ink tinted soft shell crab tempura. The meal hits its apex come sushi time when the chefs present a stack of boxes stocked with an immense selection of fish arranged by type, and then invite diners to make selections from this bounty which are then knifed into sashimi. An equally superb nigiri course follows, allowing further opportunity to delve deeper into the jaw-dropping assemblage.

■ 1503 17th St. NW (bet. Church & P Sts.)
METRO: Dupont Circle
PHONE: 202-462-8999 — **WEB:** www.sushitaro.com
■ Lunch Mon – Fri   Dinner Mon - Sat   **PRICE: $$$$**

TABARD INN

AMERICAN

   MAP: 1-C2

The Tabard Inn has history in the bag; this place is the oldest continuously operating hotel in the city. But before you assume it's just for the blue hair set, take a look at the surprisingly hip crowd who frequent it—and then join them.

Begin with a cocktail in the lounge before heading to the dining room, where the American-focused menu suits the space to a tee. There are a few outliers, like *muhammara* and house-made hummus, but the selections definitely skew red-white-and-blue: pan-seared duck breast from Maple Leaf Farms in Indiana; sea scallops from Georges Bank; and grilled dry-aged ribeye from Iowa. Artichoke hearts double as bowls for well-seasoned and tasty crabmeat stuffing, and Louisiana gumbo is deconstructed for an unusually artful look.

■ 1739 N St. NW (bet. 17th & 18th Sts.)
METRO: Dupont Circle
PHONE: 202-331-8528 — **WEB:** www.tabardinn.com
■ Lunch & dinner daily   PRICE: $$

TABERNA DEL ALABARDERO

SPANISH

                                                          MAP: 1-B4

When times call for unapologetic, old-world formality, reserve a table at Taberna del Albardero. Regal and resplendent, with everything from the walls and fabrics to the plush carpets awash in vivid red, this is the kind of place where servers donning formal attire deliver white glove service to international dignitaries—the din of a dozen different languages weaving a kind of symphony in the background.

Madrid-native Javier Romero's menu begins with classic Spanish tapas—*patatas bravas* and *gambas al ajillo*. Edgier creations may include prawn burgers on ink-tinted buns and *arroz cremosa calabaza*, a Spanish riff on risotto with tempura-fried Blue Point oysters, butternut squash purée-flavored sauce, and a drizzle of anise liqueur.

■ 1776 I St. NW (entrance on 18th St.)
METRO: Farragut North
PHONE: 202-429-2200 — **WEB:** www.alabardero.com
■ Lunch Mon – Fri   Dinner nightly   PRICE: $$$

TABLE

CONTEMPORARY

MAP: 3-A1

Spot the olive green-painted brick façade and you've arrived at Table—a Shaw bistro with two dining rooms spread over two floors. The upstairs is intimate and inviting, with whitewashed brick walls and sleek blonde wood tables with pillow-topped benches.

Small plates with a seasonal focus are a very big deal. Choose from peekytoe crab toast with curry aioli; olive oil-poached octopus with heirloom bean salad; or perhaps veal Milanese with violet-mustard jus and pickled mustard seeds. The buckwheat crêpe, full of wilted kale, cannellini beans and garnished with pickled rhubarb, makes getting your greens oh-so-enjoyable. And golden-brown skate accompanied by cockles, lentils, grilled baby eggplant, and baba ganoush immediately calls the Mediterranean to mind.

■ 903 N St. NW (bet. 9th & 10th Sts.)
METRO: Mt Vernon Sq
PHONE: 202-588-5200 — **WEB:** www.tabledc.com
■ Lunch & dinner Tue – Sun   **PRICE: $$**

TAIL UP GOAT ✿

CONTEMPORARY

✕✕ ♿ 🐾   MAP: 2-A3

A trio of veterans from Komi and Little Serow has united to bring DC its latest hot spot. What's with the name? It reflects the Caribbean upbringing of Chef Jon Sybert's wife, Jill Tyler, as well as an island expression to differentiate between goats and sheep: tail up goat, tail down sheep.

This hip bistro welcomes diners of all stripes with a buzzing bar area where thirst quenchers like the daiquiri of the day or a hibiscus *agua fresca* call to mind sandy shores. Colorful tiles, light-colored wood furnishings, and pastel accents cement the setting's easy-breezy vibe.

Chef Sybert's menu is a stimulating work that starts off with some serious bread options. The handful of choices are unlike anything previously experienced—take for example the delightfully unorthodox crostini of grilled charred chocolate rye with salt-baked sardines, sweet butter, and pickled beets. Among the pastas, hope to find supple, richly yellow *maltagliati* dressed with fermented honey sausage, pea shoots, and breadcrumbs. Whole roasted porgy is precisely de-boned and stuffed with ramps, spinach, and capers. Lastly don't miss out on sweets, particularly the crunchy *cannolo* stuffed with lemon-scented whipped ricotta.

■ 1827 Adams Mill Rd. NW (bet. Lanier Pl. & Columbia Rd.)
PHONE: 202-986-9600
WEB: www.tailupgoat.com
■ Dinner nightly   **PRICE: $$**

THIP KHAO 😊

LAO

✗✗ 🏠   MAP: 2-B1

Having earned herself a loyal following at Bangkok Garden in Falls Church, Chef Seng Luangrath is set to wow the crowds in ever-transforming Columbia Heights.

Thip Khao's menu tempts with its sheer variety, from snacks and salads to soups, curries, and panoply of entrées. *Naem khao*, a crispy coconut rice salad, bursts with fresh and fragrant flavor, while *muu som*, cured and slow-cooked pork belly, is wonderfully fatty. The *gang deng* is delicious, its mildly spicy red chili curry dotted with tender chunks of tofu and crunchy vegetables, but it's the *knap paa* or Chilean sea bass that really stands out. Brushed with curry paste and coconut cream then grilled in a banana leaf, you'll find yourself wondering: is it dinner or a present?

■ 3462 14th St. NW (bet. Meridian Pl. & Newton St.)
METRO: Columbia Heights
PHONE: 202-387-5426 — **WEB:** www.thipkao.com
■ Lunch Wed – Sun   Dinner Wed – Mon   **PRICE: $$**

TICO

LATIN AMERICAN

✗✗ 🍽   MAP: 2-B4

It may be an offshoot of the Boston original, but Tico stands on its own two feet, thank you very much. Pulsing with energy, it fits right in with this lively U Street neighborhood. The spacious dining room's dark wood furnishings and vibrant murals create the sense of relaxing in a Latin American courtyard—and trust us, once those hibiscus margaritas arrive, the easy-breezy vibe is just beginning.

There is plenty to choose from here, including ceviche (black bass is a good choice); tacos; small plates like black risotto croquettes and lamb meatballs; as well as *plancha* items like sweet and meaty prawns or sausage (*morcilla*) and peppers. *Tres leches* cake, served very cold, closes out the rollicking good time with its silky-sweet perfection.

■ 1926 14th St. NW (bet. T & U Sts.)
METRO: U St
PHONE: 202-319-1400 — **WEB:** www.ticodc.com
■ Lunch Sat – Sun   Dinner nightly   **PRICE: $$**

TOKI UNDERGROUND

JAPANESE

✗   MAP: 8-C3

It's easy to miss Toki Underground (it's above The Pug bar). That grungy stretch could be off-putting, and inside, well, it's divey. But it's all good because it just adds to the allure. The room features mostly counter and bar seating in typical ramen style and the décor does nothing to distract diners from the main event: bowls of the steaming stuff.

Toki classic is the signature—a rich yet light broth teeming with thin noodles, pulled pork, soft-poached egg, baby spinach, and a hint of *togarashi* for just the right amount of razzle-dazzle. Other variations include Taipei curry, kimchi, red miso, and a vegetarian option. There are non-soup offerings as well, like dumplings and *tsukemen* (dipping) noodles with products sourced from local farms.

■ 1234 H St. NE (bet. 12th & 13th Sts.)
PHONE: 202-388-3086
WEB: www.tokiunderground.com
■ Lunch & dinner Mon – Sat   PRICE: ☜

TOSCA

ITALIAN

✗✗ ♿ 🕸 🍽 ⛶   MAP: 3-A3

Situated at the base of a nondescript office building, Tosca doesn't initially grab attention. But with modern sophistication and warm, vaguely old-world service, this restaurant caters to an established, moneyed crowd. It's the kind of place where wheeling and dealing over plates of homemade Italian dishes is business as usual.

Pasta is a standout, and while different variations roam Italy for inspiration, almost all share a delicious richness. *Scialatielli* drenched in a white wine-cream-sauce and served with tender rabbit-based ragù has just a hint of sweetness. Then the branzino, though simple, is expertly cooked and seasoned just enough to heighten its fresh flavor. The lengthy wine list is largely Italian, though California is well-represented.

■ 1112 F St. NW (bet. 11th & 12th Sts.)
METRO: Metro Center
PHONE: 202-367-1990 — **WEB:** www.toscadc.com
■ Lunch Mon – Fri   Dinner Mon – Sat   PRICE: $$$

2AMYS 😋

PIZZA

🍴 🍺   MAP: 6-A1

Pizza fans can't get enough of this joint and for good reason: three of its wood-fired pies are D.O.C.-certified—meaning they meet the requirements of Italy's VPN (Verace Pizza Napoletana), an association created to protect and promote the Neapolitan pizza. Under its watchful eye, the kitchen must adhere to strict guidelines on everything from ingredients to preparation, ensuring this particular trio of 'za is as classic as it gets. While regulars know to order from the exceptional small plates at the wine bar, there is much on this menu to satisfy non-conformists—like the cockle- and caper-topped *vongole* or the Etna pizza with eggplant confit and olives.

Also check out the wood-fired delights made from house-milled flour at Etto, from the same dedicated owners.

■ 3715 Macomb St. NW (38th St. & Wisconsin Ave.)
PHONE: 202-885-5700
WEB: www.2amysdc.com
■ Lunch Tue – Sun   Dinner nightly   **PRICE**: $$

VIDALIA

AMERICAN

🍴🍴🍴 🍸 🎴   MAP: 1-B2

A local fixture after a whopping two decades of impressive service, Vidalia continues to delight even the most fickle diner. For city types, the dining room's magnolia-graced walls, wine bar, and warm staff provide a much-needed respite from the haughty attitude seen elsewhere. Longstanding tenure aside, the cuisine remains of-the-moment, having finessed its style of spruced-up Southern food. The bread presentation is the very first sign that no detail is overlooked here.

Regional eats like pimento cheese are given a my-fair-lady makeover; while waffles come with chicken-fried veal sweetbreads. Other treats include a rich Low Country She-crab soup; shrimp and grits that's worlds away from the one your Pa remembers; as well as an urbanized Key Lime pie.

■ 1990 M St. NW (bet. 19th & 20th Sts.)
METRO: Farragut North
PHONE: 202-659-1990 — **WEB**: www.vidaliadc.com
■ Dinner Mon – Sat   **PRICE**: $$$$

ZAYTINYA

MEDITERRANEAN

XX ♿ 🪑 🛋 🎱 👜 🍽

MAP: 3-B3

Awash in a palette of cool blue and white with an entire wall artfully decorated with Turkish nazar ornaments (eye-shaped amulets used to ward off evil spirits), Zaytinya speaks to the ease and elegance of the Mediterranean—and indeed this restaurant offers a smorgasbord of Med-influenced flavor. Though large, the dining room is sectioned into cozy nooks, and the warm, friendly service makes it feel especially inviting.

If the look is a little bit of this and a little bit of that, so is powerhouse chef, José Andrés's meze-minded menu. Ouzo-battered catfish *skordalia* and oyster saganaki are proof that Greek influences run deep, while the wine list is especially far-reaching with bottles from Lebanon and Romania along with surprises from Greece and Turkey.

■ 701 9th St. NW (at G St.)
METRO: Gallery Pl-Chinatown
PHONE: 202-638-0800 — **WEB:** www.zaytinya.com
■ Lunch & dinner daily

PRICE: $$

MICHELIN IS CONTINUALLY INNOVATING FOR SAFER, CLEANER, MORE ECONOMICAL, MORE CONNECTED AND BETTER ALL AROUND MOBILITY.

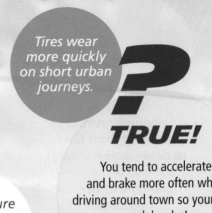

Tires wear more quickly on short urban journeys.

TRUE!

You tend to accelerate and brake more often when driving around town so your tires work harder!
If you are stuck in traffic, keep calm and drive slowly.

Tire pressure only affects your car's safety.

FALSE!

Driving with underinflated tires (0.5 below recommended pressure) doesn't just impact handling and fuel consumption, it will take 8,000 km off tire lifespan.
Make sure you check tire pressure about once a month and before you go on vacation or a long journey.

Fitting **2 winter tires** on my car guarantees maximum safety.

FALSE!

In the winter, especially when temperatures drop below 44.5°F, to ensure better road grip, all four tires should be identical and fitted at the same time.

2 WINTER TIRES ONLY =
risk of compromised road grip.

4 WINTER TIRES =
safer handling when cornering, driving downhill and braking.

If you regularly encounter rain, snow or black ice, choose a **MICHELIN Alpin tire**. This range offers you sharp handling plus a comfortable ride to safely face the challenge of winter driving.

MICHELIN IS COMMITTED

► MICHELIN IS THE **GLOBAL LEADER IN FUEL-EFFICIENT TIRES** FOR LIGHT VEHICLES.

► **EDUCATING YOUNGSTERS ON ROAD SAFETY FOR BIKES,** NOT FORGETTING TWO-WHEELERS. LOCAL ROAD SAFETY CAMPAIGNS WERE RUN IN **16 COUNTRIES** IN 2015.

QUIZ

1 TIRES ARE BLACK SO WHY IS THE MICHELIN MAN WHITE?

Back in 1898 when the Michelin Man was first created from a stack of tires, they were made of natural rubber, cotton and sulphur and were therefore light-colored. The composition of tires did not change until after the First World War when carbon black was introduced. But the Michelin Man kept his color!

2 HOW LONG HAS MICHELIN BEEN GUIDING TRAVELERS?

Since 1900. When the MICHELIN guide was published at the turn of the century, it was claimed that it would last for a hundred years. It's still around today and remains a reference with new editions and online restaurant listings in a number of countries.

3 WHEN WAS THE "BIB GOURMAND" INTRODUCED IN THE MICHELIN GUIDE?

The symbol was created in 1997 but as early as 1954 the MICHELIN guide was recommending "exceptional good food at moderate prices." Today, it features on the MICHELIN Restaurants website and app.

If you want to enjoy a fun day out and find out more about Michelin, why not visit the l'Aventure Michelin museum and shop in Clermont-Ferrand, France:
www.laventuremichelin.com

MICHELIN
A better way forward

MAPS

2

A

ROCK CREEK PARK AND
PINEY BRANCH PARKWAY

Park

Branch

Piney Rd.

Beach

NW

1

Ingleside Terr. NW

Newton St.

19th

Park St.

Klingle Rd. NW

Beach

Adams

North Rd.

Mill Rd. NW

Rock Creek

Dr. NW

MT.
PLEASANT

Rd.

Lamont St.

SMITHSONIAN

NATIONAL

2 ZOOLOGICAL

PARK

Mt. Pleasant St. NW

Kenyon St. NW

18th

Irving St. NW

Harvard St. NW

Hobart St. NW

NW

Ontario Rd. NW

Mill Rd. NW

Adams

Ontario Pl. NW

Lanier Pl. NW

WALTER PIERCE
PARK

Calvert St. NW

Beach

X X Tail Up Goat

Biltmore St. NW

X X Mintwood Place

Lapis

20th St.

Columbia Rd. NW

X X Roofers
Union

The Diner X

Sakuramen X

Mintwood Pl.
KALORAMA
PARK

8th

19th St. NW

3

ADAMS
MORGAN

Champlain St. NW

Kalorama Rd. NW

Connecticut

Kalorama

Wyoming St. NW

MARIE
REED
RECR.
CTR.
NW

Florida

X X Sushi Ogawa

Ave.

Wyoming

St. NW

Columbia

California St. NW

Vernon St. NW

X Keren

Willard St. NW

19th St. NW

California St. NW

Leroy Pl. NW

Phelps

Bancroft Pl.
NW

4

T St.
NW

20th St. NW

Swann St.
NW

X Mandu

S St.
NW

Decatur Pl. NW

Florida

Ave.

18th St. NW

Riggs
Pl. NW

New Hampshire

17th

A

St.
R

B

Spring St. NW

Spring Pl.

Perry St. NW

Ogden St. NW

14th Pl.

Brown St. NW

Newton St. NW

Meridian Pl. NW

Monroe St. NW

Otis

X X Thip Khao

NW

Park Rd. NW

16th St. NW

17th

Pleasant St. NW

X X Purple Patch

GALA
(TIVOLI
THEATER)

POWELL
RECREATION
CENTER

Hiatt St. NW

Columbia
Heights

15th St. NW

14th

Columbia Rd.

RABAUT
PARK

Harvard St.

MEXICAN
CULTURAL
INSTITUTE

COLUMBIA
HEIGHTS
PARK

COLUMBIA HEIGH

Fuller St. NW

Euclid St. NW

16th St. NW

Ontario Rd. NW

NW

Chapin St. NW

MERIDIAN
HILL
PARK

Belmont St. NW

Belmont St. NW

Florida

X X Kapnos

V St. NW

Jack Rose
Dining Saloon X X

U St.
NW

Ave.

X X Tico

X X Lupo Verde

Hampshire

Swann St. NW

Doi Moi X X

14th

15th St.

16th St.

17th St. NW

New

Pl. NW

B St.
R

NW

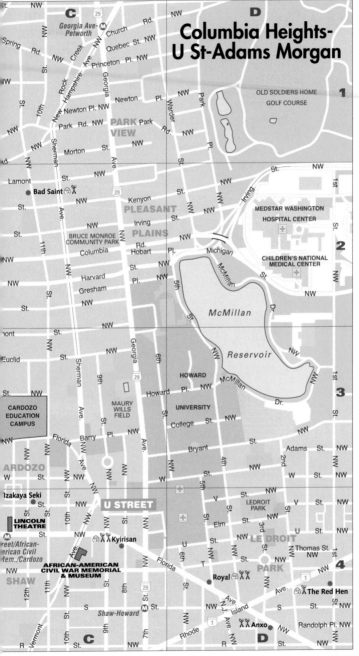

Columbia Heights-
U St-Adams Morgan

C

D

1

29

Georgia Ave-
Petworth

Church Rd.

Quebec St. NW

Princeton Pl. NW

Spring Rd.

Rock Creek

New Hampshire Ave.

NW

10th St.

NW

Georgia Ave.

Newton Pl. NW

Newton Pl.

NW

Warder St.

Park Rd.

OLD SOLDIERS HOME
GOLF COURSE

Park Rd. NW

Park Rd.

**PARK
VIEW**

Morton St.

NW

NW

Sherman Ave.

Lamont St.

NW

● Bad Saint ✗

29

Kenyon St.

St.

NW

Irving St.

NW

Irving St.

NW

1st St.

St. NW

**MEDSTAR WASHINGTON
HOSPITAL CENTER**

✚

2

PLEASANT

St.

11th St.

NW

NW

PLAINS

**BRUCE MONROE
COMMUNITY PARK**

Columbia Rd.

Hobart Pl.

NW

Michigan

**CHILDREN'S NATIONAL
MEDICAL CENTER**

✚

NW

1st St. NW

NW

Harvard St.

NW

Gresham Pl.

NW

St.

5th St.

NW

McMillan Dr.

St.

NW

mont St.

NW

Euclid St.

NW

Sherman Ave.

9th St.

NW

Georgia

29

6th St.

NW

McMillan

Reservoir

NW

NW

3

NW

St. NW

**CARDOZO
EDUCATION
CAMPUS**

Florida Ave.

Barry Pl.

N NW

NW

**MAURY
WILLS
FIELD**

Howard Pl. NW

HOWARD

UNIVERSITY

College St.

NW

McMillan Dr.

4th St.

Bryant St.

NW

Adams St. NW

2nd St. NW

1st St.

ARDOZO

W St.

NW

5th St.

W St.

NW

● Izakaya Seki

St.

10th St.

NW

NW

St. NW

V St.

St.

**LEDROIT
PARK**

V St. NW

3rd St. NW

LE DROIT

U St.

NW

1st St.

■ **LINCOLN
THEATRE**

Elm St.

St.

U St.

NW

🚇 reet/African-
erican Civil
Mem./Cardozo

NW

♿✗ Kyirisan

6th St.

T St.

NW

Thomas St.
NW

PARK

NW

SHAW

**AFRICAN-AMERICAN
CIVIL WAR MEMORIAL
& MUSEUM**

8th St.

29

Florida Ave.

St.

Royal ♿✗ ●

1

♿✗ ● **The Red Hen**

4

12th St.

NW

Vermont

10th St.

St.

🚇 M St.

Shaw-Howard

7th St.

S St.

Ave.

NJ

Island Ave.

1

NW

✗ Anxo

Randolph Pl. NW

NW

R St.

Rhode

R St.

NW

D

St.

NW

C

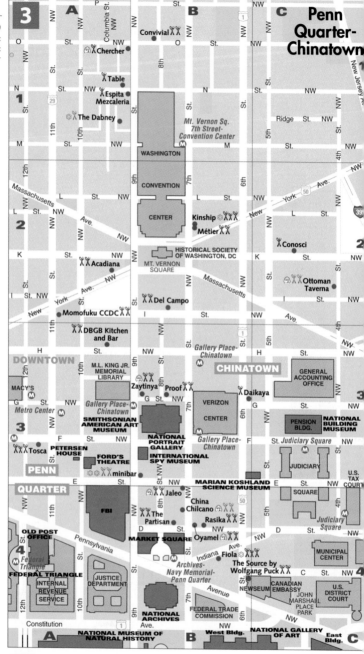

3

A NW

P St.

Columbia St. NW

8th St. NW

B NW

C Penn Quarter-Chinatown

New Jersey

Convivial ✕✕

St. NW

Chercher ⊕✕

O St. NW

1

Ridge St. NW

Table ✕

Espita Mezcaleria ✕

29

The Dabney ⊕✕

Mt. Vernon Sq. 7th Street-Convention Center

N St. NW

N St.

5th St. NW

4th NW

WASHINGTON

12th St.

Massachusetts

Ave. NW

L St. NW

9th St.

7th

CONVENTION

CENTER

6th St. NW

York 50 Ave.

New L St. NW

39

2

M St. NW

MT. VERNON SQUARE

Kinship ⊕✕✕

Métier ✕✕

Conosci ✕

2

HISTORICAL SOCIETY OF WASHINGTON, DC

Massachusetts Ave.

K St. NW

Acadiana ✕✕

St. NW

Ottoman Taverna ⊕✕✕

I St. NW

York St. NW

New

Del Campo ✕✕

St. NW

5th

4th

Momofuku CCDC ✕✕

DBGB Kitchen and Bar ✕✕

Ave.

NW

11th

10th

Gallery Place-Chinatown

St. NW

1

St.

H St. NW

5th NW

DOWNTOWN

12th

M.L. KING JR. MEMORIAL LIBRARY

CHINATOWN

GENERAL ACCOUNTING OFFICE

MACY'S G

10th

Zaytinya ⊕✕✕

Proof ✕✕

VERIZON CENTER

Daikaya ✕

G St. NW

Metro Center G

St. NW

Gallery Place-Chinatown

7th

6th

PENSION BLDG.

NATIONAL BUILDING MUSEUM

3

SMITHSONIAN AMERICAN ART MUSEUM

NATIONAL PORTRAIT GALLERY

Gallery Place-Chinatown

F

St. Judiciary Square NW

✕✕✕Tosca

PETERSEN HOUSE

INTERNATIONAL SPY MUSEUM

JUDICIARY

PENN

FORD'S THEATRE

minibar ⊕✕

MARIAN KOSHLAND SCIENCE MUSEUM

E St. NW

U.S. TAX COURT

QUARTER

11th

FBI

Jaleo ⊕✕

China Chilcano ⊕✕✕

50

SQUARE

4th

Judiciary Square

OLD POST OFFICE

Pennsylvania

The Partisan ✕✕

Rasika ⊕✕✕

D St. NW

MUNICIPAL CENTER

Federal Triangle

JUSTICE DEPARTMENT

MARKET SQUARE

Oyamel ⊕✕✕

Indiana Ave.

Fiola ✕✕✕

C St. NW

4

FEDERAL TRIANGLE

INTERNAL REVENUE SERVICE

10th

Archives-Navy Memorial-Penn Quarter

NEWSEUM

The Source by Wolfgang Puck ✕✕

CANADIAN EMBASSY

JOHN MARSHALL PLACE PARK

U.S. DISTRICT COURT

12th

Constitution

1

NATIONAL MUSEUM OF NATURAL HISTORY

NATIONAL ARCHIVES

7th

FEDERAL TRADE COMMISSION

Avenue

6th NW

NATIONAL GALLERY OF ART

East Bldg.

Ave.

NW

A

B West Bldg.

C

A   B   C

JOHN ADAMS
BUILDING

LIBRARY
OF
CONGRESS

Independence   SE   SE   SE

**Near
Southeast**

Capitol
Hill   Ave.   SE

5th
St.   SE

ⲬⲬ Sonoma   Pennsylvania   Seward Sq. SE   EASTERN
MARKET   SE   SE   SE

JAMES
MADISON
BUILDING   SEWARD   C   St.   SE   C   St.   SE   **1**

C   St.   4th St.   SQUARE   6th St.

1   Seward Sq. SE   St.   St.

D   St.   SE   Carolina   Ave.   7th   8th St.   9th St.   South Carolina Ave.

North   St.   3rd St.   FOLGER
SQUARE   St.   St.   SE   Eastern
Market Ⓜ   D St. SE   10th St.   SE

D   SE   MARKET   PARK   D   St.   SE

E   St.   5th St.   Ave.   SE   D   St.   SE   SE   SE

2nd St.   St.   SE   Ave.   Ⲭ Eatbar   E   SE   SE

iddington
Pl.   Carolina   MARION PARK   E   St.   SE

South   SE   SE   Ⲭ Ambar   St.   **2**

St. SE   4th St.   4th St.   St.   Ⲭ Cava Mezze   ● Garrison ⲬⲬ

GARFIELD   PARK   3rd St.   G   St.   SE   St.   St.   St.   SE

NEAR   ❀ⲬⲬ Pineapple
and Pearls   MARINE
BARRACKS

St. SE   Virginia   5th St.   Ellen Wilson Pl.   ❀Ⲭ Rose's
Luxury   7th   8th St.   9th St.   10th St.

695   Virginia   Ave.   SE   St.   SE

SE   SE   SOUTHEAST   Virginia   I   St.   SE   695

I   St.   SE   SE   SE   SE   Ave.   FREEWAY

SOUTHEAST   VIRGINIA
AVENUE
PARK

K   St.   St.   SE   SE   SE   SE

WASHINGTON   3rd Pl.   St.   L   St.   St.   L St. SE   **3**

3   CANAL   St.   St.   SE

PARK   2nd St.   3rd St.   4th St.   5th St.   7th   8th St.   9th St.

jersey   M   St.   SE   M   St.   SE

Navy Yard-
Ballpark   U.S. DEPARTMENT
OF
TRANSPORTATION   Warrington   Ave.   Parsons

Ave.   SE   SE   Isaac St.   Patterson   Dahlgren   10th St.

St. SE   Tingey   St.   Tingey   St.   SE   Hull St.   Ave.   Paulding   NAVY   N   St.

St. SE   3rd St.   4th St.   WASHINGTON   Ave.   NAVY   YARD

Pl. SE   ⲬⲬ Due South   Water St. SE   ● Osteria Morini ⲬⲬ   Bowen St.   NAVY
MUSEUM   Paulding Ave.   Ave.   O   St.

St. SE   THE YARDS
PARK   SE   Sicard St. SE   SE   SE   **4**

ANACOSTIA   RIVER

A   B   C

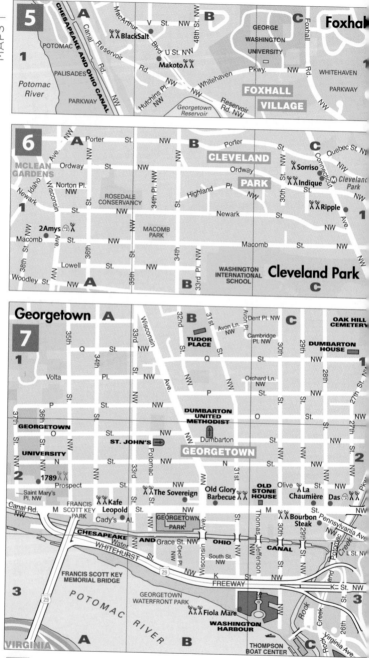

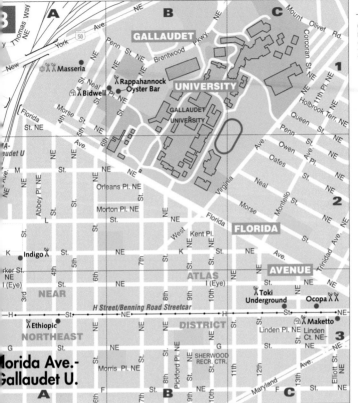

INDEX
OF RESTAURANTS

CREDITS

Page 2 up: ©Michelin / H. SOTO ▪ Page 2 down: ©Michelin / GF ▪ Page 5 up: ©Michelin / H. SOTO ▪ Page 5 down: ©Michelin / H. SOTO ▪ Page 7: ©Michelin / Elena Mehlman ▪ Pages 10-11: ©Michelin / GF ▪ Page 16: ©Michelin / Jeanine Hart ▪ Page 21: ©Michelin / AS ▪ Page 29: ©Michelin / H. SOTO ▪ Page 31: ©Michelin / Jeanine Hart ▪ Page 33: ©Michelin / M. Chiesa ▪ Page 38: ©Michelin / AS ▪ Page 45: ©Michelin / H. SOTO ▪ Page 47: ©Michelin / H. SOTO ▪ Page 54: ©Michelin / H. SOTO ▪ Page 55: ©Michelin / H. SOTO ▪ Page 61: ©Michelin / H. SOTO ▪ Page 67: ©Michelin / AS ▪ Page 70: ©Michelin / AS

Michelin Travel Partner
Société par actions simplifiées au capital de 11 288 880 EUR
27 Cours de l'Île Seguin - 92100 Boulogne Billancourt (France)
R.C.S. Nanterre 433 677 721
© Michelin et Cie, Propriétaires-Éditeurs 2016

Printed in Canada - septembre 2016, on paper from sustainably managed forests.
Compogravure : Nord Compo à Villeneuve d'Ascq (France)
Impression et Finition : Transcontinental (Canada)

3 1170 01015 9360